Carbon Copies: Shadows of the Almighty

By R. Harris

Carbon Copies Shadows of the Almighty by R. Harris
Published by RyDeas LLC
Copyright © 2024 by R.Harris All rights reserved

Print ISBN: 979-8-9923405-0-1
E-Book ISBN: 979-8-9923405-1-8
Audiobook available on Google Play Books, GGKEY:KRWN94WBP8T

No part of this book may be reproduced without permission from the publisher. No part of this book may be transmitted or stored in any form by any means without permission from the publisher.
For inquiries email - R.HarrisWrites@gmail.com

Cover design by R. Harris
Follow on social media: R.HarrisWrites

You can find more information about the author, current works, and upcoming projects on the R. Harris website: RHarrisWrites.com

SCAN HERE FOR

R.HARRIS WRITES
WEBSITE

Contents

Preface 5
   The Purpose 5
Introduction 7
   Structure of the Book 7
In Reality 10
   Dimensions 13
   Where's Your Mind? 18
   Time 25
      Chapter Reflection: In Reality 31
In-Plane Sight 34
   Spaces 35
   Groups 40
   Know Your Role 44
   Misguided Guidance 48
   Work & Play 53
      Chapter Reflection: In-Plane Sight 57
Our Voice 61
   Expression & Expectation 62
   Wakes to Waves 70
   Love Who? 73
   Love Is 78
   Love Unlimited 86
   True or False 90
      Chapter Reflection: Our Voice 98
The Void 103
   Fertile Ground 104
   The Search 107
   Follow Freely 111
   Follow Filled 121
      Chapter Reflection: The Void 128

Contents

Confused Communication...**131**
   Designed Division... 135
   Deflection... 146
   On the Contrary... 152
   Blurred Vision.. 156
   The Ear of the Beholder................................... 164
     Chapter Reflection: Confused Communication........167

The Problem with Evolution is… Humans........................**171**
   In the Beginning...172
   Are We There Yet?... 176
   New & Improved.. 180
   Design & Development..................................... 183
   Plot Twist.. 186
     Chapter Reflection: The Problem with Evolution is… Humans... 190

Carbon Copies..**191**
   Sowing Seeds...194
     Chapter Reflection: Carbon Copies......................... 201

Just a Man..**203**
   Fighting Against Flesh...................................... 203
   Fire and Brimstone.. 211
   In All Fairness..213
   Good, Bad, & Other... 216
     Chapter Reflection: Just a Man............................... 224

More Than a Man..**227**
   Three and One... 231
   New Navigation... 243
   True North..246
   Calibrated Compass.. 254
   Light & Death.. 269
   Plain and Simple..271
     Chapter Reflection: More Than a Man.....................275

Book Reflection... 279

Epilogue.. **280**
    The Book Title..280
    Receiving Salvation..282
    The Writing Process... 284
    About the Author..287
    Share Your Thoughts...288

Preface

The Purpose

This book was written to encourage people to consider God in their experiences. It is my hope that as readers walk through the text, they examine themselves physically, mentally, and spiritually with a biblical lens. This examination should not be led by a mindset or heart posture of criticism, but with the intent to seek understanding about oneself, God, and the world around them.

The content surveys what we perceive as reality, our independent experiences, our collective experiences, and what we cannot fully perceive as human beings. It sheds light on the things in this world that can distract individuals and mankind from its purpose. It is encouragement to start or continue an active relationship with God the Father, Jesus Christ, and the Holy Spirit.

Being in an active relationship with God is an eternal, personal journey. This journey is personal because God knows you by your name and has crafted many things within you. Your true identity and purpose can only be realized and drawn out by the one that created you. To help us seek and get to know Him, He has given the world the Holy Bible. The Word of GOD which is made known through the Bible is alive and was sent to reconcile mankind with God.

Love, structure, and peace beyond our understanding are eternal promises that can only be fulfilled by God through Jesus Christ. It is my hope that these writings equip people with a fresh perspective of God, the world, and themselves.

Introduction

The human experience reaches beyond the tangible. Thoughts, emotions, and desires are intangible components that reside in the mystery of consciousness, and enter the world through action. Our perspective of reality is formed through combining these internal elements with a multitude of external factors. Considering the pace and volume of inputs individuals experience in modern societies, is it possible that in being hyperactive our senses have become oversaturated? What if we've become so numb and indifferent that we do not fully perceive or process our personal experiences? A fresh perspective can give new insight to astray presumptions.

Structure of the Book

Considering the personal journey of readers, each chapter of the book has subsections that tie into the overall theme of the chapter. The goal is to encourage readers to process each subsection at a pace that fosters self reflection. At the end of each chapter there are questions that were created to prompt readers to consider the subjects based on their personal experiences. The answers are for self reflection purposes and do not have to be shared with anyone.

Throughout the book there is **bold text** that references biblical scripture (written in parentheses). The bold texts are not direct quotes from the Bible. They can be interpretations and/or applications of the referenced material. It is strongly encouraged for readers to read and study the entire Bible for themselves. There is no book that can replace, substitute, improve, or be held next to the Holy Bible; it is sufficient. Having the heart and mind to humbly seek God is a key component in unpacking and digesting spiritual content.

I hope and pray that this book encourages others to seek clarity regarding their identity. Clarity comes at the cost of being truthful, vulnerable, and persistent. In summary, here are the fundamental questions that are asked throughout the book:

- ❖ What are your experiences?
- ❖ What is influencing your perception?
- ❖ What does the Bible say about you and your experiences?

Make no mistake, the God of Abraham is God.

God sent His son, Jesus Christ, so we can be forgiven of our sins and show us how to live in love. The Holy Spirit is the Spirit of God that is here to help us navigate life on Earth.

Chapter 1
In Reality

If you have spent time reading books, watching TV, scrolling through your smartphone, or playing video games, it's safe to say that you have a relationship with two-dimensional (2-D) worlds. Paintings, drawings, photography, film, and digital creations are forms of expression that can be presented in 2-D.

What is interesting to me about these creations is that they do not have to represent what is "real" in our world, but can directly influence our perspective of the world. They all have the potential to inspire an individual or spark a collective movement. This observation made me think about what reality is, how we perceive it, and the things we do or do not acknowledge about it.

What is our immediate reality? Our immediate reality is this three-dimensional (3-D) world. We have length, height, and depth. What are drawings, pictures, and videos? They are two dimensional creations (length and height). So, 3-D beings can create works in 2-D, and 2-D creations can influence the 3-D world. This is important because it allows us to recognize a relationship between the two worlds.

The relationship is that 3-D has authority over 2-D, but 3-D can give 2-D the power of influence in the 3-D world. The ability to communicate can only be established by the 3-D beings, but both worlds can cross-communicate after initialization. A notable takeaway is that works in 2-D most likely cannot fully perceive the 3-D world even though it can have significant influence in that world.

We experience a similar hierarchical relationship that the 2-D world has with the 3-D world. The spiritual world is like a world that is of a higher dimension. I am not stating that the spiritual world is literally a higher dimension. I believe describing it as a higher dimension is the easiest way to digest the concept. In this book the term "dimension" will be used to describe the "level" of natural and spiritual worlds.

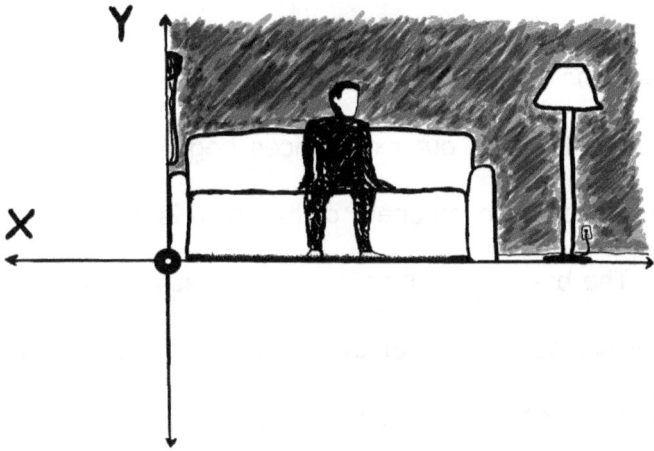

Scene drawn in a 2-Dimensions, (X,Y) coordinate system

Same scene as above drawn in a 3-Dimension (X,Y, Z) coordinate system. Notice the significant increase in information available compared to the 2-D version

13 In Reality

Dimensions

As humans our experiences begin in the mind. The flesh and blood component of the mind is what we call the brain. The brain is commonly perceived as nothing more than a physical component of the body, but as we explore and reflect on our human experiences, I believe that we will learn there is more to the brain than its physical functions.

Physically, the brain receives and sends signals through electrical and chemical interactions throughout the body. It tells the body how to operate internally and how to interact with its surroundings. Our physical, emotional, and intellectual experiences are received, processed, and evaluated through the brain. With modern technology a brain can be supplied with everything it needs on a physical level to make it function. Yet, that is not enough to make a brain conscious. When a brain is not able to be conscious the person is considered to be deceased.

If fulfilling the brain's physical requirements is not enough for a person to be declared as a living being, then there has to be more to the brain than just the physical aspect. I believe this is an indicator that there is a non-physical component that leads the brain. The key component that gives the brain and subsequently rest of the body life is the soul.

The soul is the source of life and consciousness for humans. Souls can be viewed as the spiritual version of the brain. Our soul is where our thoughts, desires, and emotions get processed and reside spiritually. How these combined categories are processed and expressed can be summarized as an individual's identity. So how we express ourselves can reveal to us and others, the things we identify with. Our identity is found in our soul.

The soul does not reside in this world, it is a spiritual creation. Because it is a spiritual creation, it is superior to its flesh and blood counterpart, the brain. One of the ways that the soul is superior to the brain is that it is eternal. **The soul is what ties our physical and spiritual bodies together** even though they are of different "dimensions" (1 Thessalonians 5:23). When I say bodies (plural), I am speaking about our physical body and our spiritual body. **Each person has two bodies** when they are born into this world (1 Corinthians 15:42-44).

A spiritual body is what it sounds like. Humans have a spiritual body or vessel that resides in the spiritual world. Because that body is created in and for a place that is of a higher "dimension," it is greater than its flesh and blood counterpart. We cannot "naturally" fully perceive our spiritual body similar in the way 2-D creations cannot fully perceive the 3-D world. We may not visually perceive our soul or spirit in these 3-D bodies, but they are just as real as anything on Earth. To clarify, that "higher dimension" transcends ours in reference to what is considered "real."

Our spiritual body also experiences inputs just like our physical bodies. Without being spiritually aware our sensitivity to our spirit will be low (numb). This could be a reason why spirituality in general is rejected by some. With the soul being at the center of our physical and spiritual bodies, it receives inputs from both sides. Our worldly thoughts, desires, and emotions meet with their spiritual counterparts in the soul. It is our soul that makes the ultimate choice of what we identify with and the outward expressions of that identity.

Considering the "position" and relationship between the physical and spiritual worlds, I was led to the conclusion that for us to have a better understanding of this 3-D world, we have to acknowledge that we are spiritual beings with souls. I believe this acknowledgement will bring fresh perspectives and a clearer understanding of who we are as individuals and as a species.

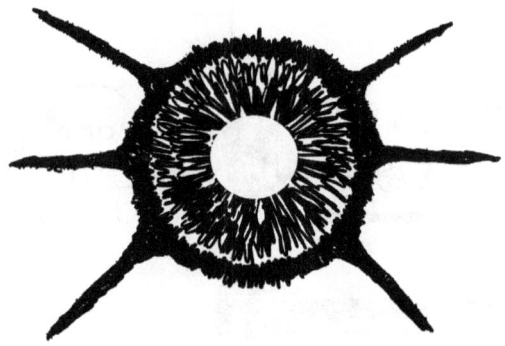

The Soul: Connects humans to the earthly and spiritual worlds

17 In Reality

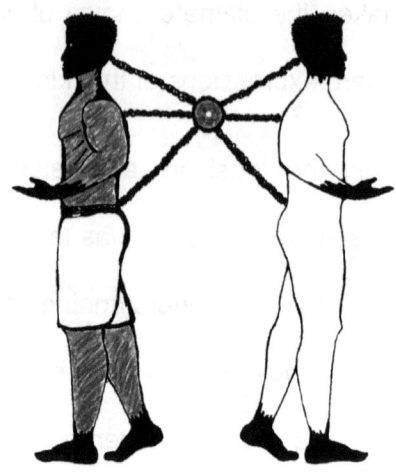

Tethered: Physical body (left) & spiritual body (right) connected by the soul (center)

The physical world (left), unable to perceive what inhabits the spiritual world (right)

Where's Your Mind?

The word "mind" is a descriptor of the brain and soul collaboration. When people choose to fully lead their bodies with their minds, some extraordinary occurrences can take place. Many people experience situations where the mind had to "overlook" what the body was experiencing in order to survive or complete a seemingly impossible task. These occurrences can include situations where extremely high endurance or strength is required. "Hysterical Strength" and "Survival Instinct" are common terms when these events take place.

These feats are indicators that the mind has authority over the body. That may seem obvious, but many allow their physical body or circumstance to limit their ability to discern and overcome situations. Logic suggests that for optimum results in this 3-D world one should think spiritually first, and use that information to lead their physical expressions. It would be optimal because the spirit is from a higher "dimension." Which means it can have access to greater perspectives, increased sensitivity, and improved authority in regard to its surroundings.

So, to be our "best" selves, our body should follow our mind and our mind should reference our spirit. Which leads to these questions: What are you doing with your body? What is your mind focused on? and what state is your spirit in?

If your mind is following your flesh, then you most likely experience feelings of emptiness, confusion, and internal conflict relatively frequently. In other words, you find yourself doing things or in places that you don't morally agree with, enjoy, or find fulfilling. This is because you are allowing the lesser (flesh) to lead the greater (spirit).

How many times have you "woken up" from a situation and asked yourself, "How did I get here?"? Often that question comes with little to no understanding or logic to why you chose to do things that went against your better judgment. Drinking too much, the embarrassing "morning after," and unnecessary fighting are a few symptoms of following your flesh.

Those situations are the result of being mentally and spiritually lost. In terms of awareness and intelligence, flesh is the least capable part of us. When the flesh leads, mental, spiritual, and physical health is subject to higher risks. That does not mean you won't experience "bad" situations when you are mentally and spiritually aware. It means you will know how you got "here," and can make sense of the logic and choices you've made that yielded the results before you.

If your mind is leading your flesh, but you're only looking at this 3-D world, then you're not using your spiritual "view" to direct your mind. This means you're lacking in understanding and perception. The higher dimension will always have a better "view" of what's going on. Even when a person has a great understanding of this world, they are functioning by a fraction of their being. Operating in the higher dimension will grant access to higher levels of perception and understanding.

Beings that are spiritually aware will have some advantages over beings that are not. For example, influence is spiritual in nature, but many do not identify it as a spiritual component. Being influenced by someone or something without understanding their spiritual nature can lead to negative situations. This is why God told us to **live by the spirit and not by the flesh** (Galatians 5:16-26). He does not want us to live blind, confused, or conflicted. God knows what would give us love, peace, and fulfillment, and He does not want us to follow things that will lead to our destruction.

Considering the reality that the flesh and the mind can be misleading, your next questions may be: If I'm supposed to be led by my spirit, how can I follow or have influence on something that I cannot perceive? How can I be sure that the direction is good?

Let's talk about virtual reality (VR). Current VR technology is so cleverly designed that you can put on reactive gear and feel things in that virtual world. You can hold something in that 2-D world and it can physically manifest a reaction in your 3-D body. It can have an influence on you, it can resist you, it can encourage you, it can slow you down or speed you up. It can also influence how you think and feel. Here's the thing, just like that virtual world was cleverly designed to have influence on your mind and body, you were cleverly designed to have influence beyond what you can fully comprehend. **Your physical body can have influence on your spiritual body** and the spiritual world (1 Corinthians 6:15-20).

In terms of knowing if a direction is good, we are going to continue referencing VR. The VR world doesn't really know what is happening outside of itself. The only way it can know what is happening outside of its virtual environment is by the user inputs.

In our situation, we are in the VR world. We really don't know what is happening outside of our dimension. What that means is without spiritual guidance, we are operating solely in a reactive capacity to whatever is happening in the spiritual world. That means we could be open to random "users" inputting whatever they want into our lives, and there are no solid points of reference to know which way we are oriented.

In Reality

So, to get properly oriented and moving with our spiritual self, we need a being that is above us in every way. A being from a higher dimension, a higher level, someone that has higher authority, higher insight, and higher understanding. We need this guide so our spirit can be in a good position. Yielding to a higher authority can put our spirit in a good place, which could put our mind in a good place, which could put us as beings in a good place across the board.

Our creator, **The God of Abraham** (Galatians 3:6-9), is the only one that is good to have as your spiritual guide. He is a being that is **willing to save every single person from perishing** (2 Peter 3:9). He is the only being that has the ability to **give His only son as a sacrifice to save all of mankind** (John 3:16-17). Our goal should be to have God as our one and only spiritual guide.

I want to bring up a point of how this 3-D world is less than the spiritual in terms of ability. There are very talented artists that can draw something where it is very difficult to tell that it is not real, but it is not. This style of art is called hyperrealism. These works of art capture the characteristics of the 3-D world in great detail. They can stir emotions and provoke thoughts. If you're not paying attention, they can fool you into thinking that they are 3-D creations. But, if you have the mind to take a step back, you will see that these drawings are less than, unequal, and of a lower authority than what they represent in this 3-D world.

God said **we are created in His image** (Genesis 1:26). In order for us to be led by His spirit, we have to acknowledge that we are less than Him in every way. If we don't acknowledge His existence, if we view ourselves as equals or just flat-out rebel against Him, we cannot follow Him. God is the artist; we are His artwork. His desire is for us to be close to Him. **We have to follow His lead** for that to happen (John 10:7-10). We need Him, He doesn't need us. His guidance is available to us because of His matchless, patient, and faithful love.

Even when we are at our worst God's love doesn't waiver. Constantly working and calling out to everyone. Waiting for that fraction of a second when we're willing to listen so He can step in and help. When we let His spirit guide ours, we will be a complete, beautiful work of art. We will not self-destruct. He will reveal who, what, and where we are supposed to be. Even if we deviate at times, He has no problem with nudging us so we can get back on track. It's a matter of us acknowledging who the creator is, knowing our position as the created, and **following His instruction** to the best of our abilities (Hebrews 4:14-16).

Time

Time can be given and taken, fully used, or fully wasted. It's one of the few things that everyone is born with. Is it distributed evenly? Not in this world. Do we know how much time we have as individuals? Absolutely not. That is one of the reasons why it's so valuable. We know it is limited, we know we cannot buy it, and we know that **once it's spent, it is spent** (Ecclesiastes 8:8).

It's important to understand that humans do not fully understand dimensions. For our own comprehension we use labels and numbers. The labels, definitions, and numerical order of dimensions are not likely "law" anywhere outside of mankind. One might consider time as the 4th dimension, which is possible. It may be the only thing from a "higher dimension" that we collectively acknowledge and use every day. We experience it, it affects us, and yet we have no control over it. The only thing we can do with time is manage how we spend it.

We also have a simplified understanding of time because **we cannot fully perceive time** (2 Peter 3:8). Days that seem "long" or "short," things moving in "slow motion" at epic moments, enjoyable events where "time flies by," and miserable situations that "last forever," are ways we experience our limited perception of time. Of all the things we have, time is the second most valuable possession of humans. **Our soul is the most valuable** (Matthew 16:26).

So why do people give their time to people and things that don't add true value to their life? Because they place value in the wrong things. No, I can't tell you what you should deem valuable now. I can tell you that when your time is close to being spent you will know the things you willingly wasted your time on.

This is a reason why **respecting your elders is important** (1 Peter 5:5). Not every elder will be wise, but you may learn from their lifetime worth of experiences. Surveying someone else's experiences can save you from wasting your time. People can become reluctant to share their experiences if they don't feel heard or respected.

With the understanding that time operates on a higher "dimension" and is valuable to us, it would be logical and wise to seek guidance on how to spend our time. The wise and logical thing to do when choosing guidance would be to seek counsel from a being that is of a higher "dimension" than time. A being that has unfathomable understanding and complete authority over time would be the perfect guide. The logical and wise thing to do would be to look to God because not only does He check all the ability requirements, **He also greatly values you** (Luke 15:8-10).

In order to receive guidance, you have to take the time to ask. How much time have you wasted doing things you thought were a good use of your time? How much space and/or time do you consciously give to God so He can guide you? How many unqualified people do you run to for direction? Familiarity, age, academic education, and title are things that do not grant wisdom. A wise word from a stranger can become a compass that guides you through many situations in life. That is why wisdom is so highly valued, but unfortunately it is misunderstood.

Wisdom can only be obtained spiritually. It is not something that comes solely from learning and/or from time passing. There are many "smart" people that are not wise, just like there are many aged people that are not wise. **Wisdom is a spirit that is given by God, and He gives it liberally** (Proverbs 4:6, 8:12; James 1:5).

When you seek truth with a humble heart, when you use your ears more than your mouth, when you try to keep peace more than disturb it, you are welcoming the spirit of God into your presence. **The spirit of God brings** several **provisions**, including wisdom (James 1:17).

It is common for people to ask God for things that they think should be the provision. It should be understood that in most cases we do not fully understand our situations. Operating by our own understanding causes us to stumble, struggle, and as a result, waste time. Seeking guidance from God on how to use your time will be time well spent. Asking God for wisdom will add to your understanding of many things, including where to seek counsel. Proper counsel will save you time and potentially bless you with wisdom.

When you seek guidance from God, ask God what He wants you to do. Ask plainly, honestly, and if possible, ask in private (Matthew 6:5-8). We are easily distracted creatures. Whenever asking questions (in the flesh or spirit), it is wise to listen to what is said instead of listening for what we want to hear. Remember, no matter where you are, you can ask God for wisdom or help directly, "Lord Jesus, please guide me." When we want to communicate with God, we **pray in the name of Jesus Christ** because that is our instruction (John 14:12-14).

God says **He is the beginning and the end** (Revelation 22:13). We cannot fathom the extent of dimensions and realms He has created. The reality is that He stands outside of them all. Though our brains cannot fully process that, it's ok because He is here and happy to guide us. A child does not fully understand or comprehend what's going on around them, so they have to rely on an adult to not only survive, but also thrive.

Mankind is in a similar situation. **We need to rely on God** (Matthew 18:3-4). That's why He says He is our Father in Heaven. The parallels between this world and the spiritual world are pretty plain to see if you take the time to look.

Chapter Reflection: In Reality

Dimensions

- ❖ Have you ever considered that the soul is real? If so, where do you think your soul is?
- ❖ In your day-to-day actions, have you considered how you are impacted by the physical and spiritual "worlds"?

Where's Your Mind?

- ❖ In this season of your life, what are you doing with your body?
- ❖ What has your mind been focused on?
- ❖ What state is your spirit in?
- ❖ Is there a scenario in your life where you feel like you were led by your body? Were you happy with the result?
- ❖ Have you experienced situations or seasons where you prioritized your mind over your body? Were you happy with the result?
- ❖ Have you ever felt led by a spirit? What was that like?

- Would you have changed what you let lead you?
- Do you feel that you allow people to lead you or do you feel like you have to have control?
- How often do you give something control in your life?
- Have you ever felt that there were other "users" influencing your life at times?
- Do you acknowledge God's existence? Why?
- Have you ever asked God to lead you? If so, in what context? If not, why?

Time

- What are some things you willingly waste and/or have wasted your time on?
- What measures do you think are needed to change the habit of wasting time?
- Is there a situation where you wish you had listened to an elder?
- Is there a moment you wish lasted a little bit longer?
- Do you think you ask unqualified people for guidance and/or direction?

33 In Reality

- ❖ Do you ever get distracted when praying or asking God for guidance?
- ❖ How much time and space (free reign) do you consciously give to God so He can guide you?

Chapter 2
In-Plane Sight

Experiences in this world can give insight to how the spiritual world operates fundamentally. Most societies subscribe to a type of hierarchy where laws and figures of authority are widely recognized (relatively). These systems of organization can be observed from a global scale all the way down to a single family. A wide variety of creatures and places interact, which yields dynamic environments and experiences. Personal and shared spaces can influence beyond comprehension.

These are all a glimpse into the spiritual world. God can grant the ability to see spiritual things plainly within our worldly viewing plane. An individual's willingness to see is often the limiting factor for receiving the ability to see.

In-Plane Sight

Spaces

Spaces are very significant. A space can influence and reflect everything about a person's being. Objects, shapes, materials, light, darkness, smells, and sounds are all things that are significant in the occupation and experience of a space. Also, people within a space, whether they are familiar or unfamiliar, can dramatically change an experience. The spaces we are exposed to are significant because spaces can have a spiritual influence.

It's important to understand that just like we have our personal space on earth, we have a personal space in the spiritual world. From the previous chapter we have some understanding that the earth and our physical bodies are more or less subordinate versions of the spiritual world. So now we can try to visualize some things.

Look at the room or space that you are in. I want you to imagine that it has its own atmosphere, a bubble that whatever is in it can directly affect you, good or bad. Now, depending on where you are, there may be people, things, or other creatures that can enter that bubble and have direct access to you. Knowing that we are spiritual beings, I want you to understand that many things have spiritual versions of themselves too. You cannot see or interact directly with their "spiritual versions" with your physical body, but they are spiritually significant. This can apply to "inanimate" objects and living things.

There are also beings that mostly operate in the spiritual world similarly to how humans mostly operate in this world. These beings can be good or bad. It's important to understand that "good" is defined by God, and is only good if God calls it good (I will expand on this topic in a later chapter). The good beings aren't a problem because they're good, but the bad, it's self explanatory.

Interacting with bad or unclean spirits directly or indirectly can be problematic in ways that aren't as obvious as interacting with a "bad" person. The interactions are different because they are spiritual entities. **You cannot defend your spirit against them on your own** (Ephesians 6:12-13). That means **everything in our physical space should be**

considered to have some level of spiritual significance (Exodus 40:9-11).

Looking back to the 2-D, 3-D, and virtual reality examples, we can deduce that what we do in this world can have influence on the spiritual world. So, what we do, the people we hang out with, the spaces we create or put ourselves into, all have the potential to have an effect on our spirit and its "atmosphere." With that understanding we can conclude that where we are can directly affect our mind, body, and spirit simultaneously. This means the mind and the physical being can reflect what the spirit has been exposed to and vice versa.

With a mind and physical body influenced, the being can create a space in this world that reflects its spiritual state. This can create a cycle of influence. That cycle can be good or bad. A cycle can go like this: As a spiritual space gets exposed to bad things, the physical space becomes exposed to bad things. This then allows the spiritual space to become surrounded by more bad things. Which will influence the physical space to be surrounded by bad things. Eventually, both spaces will be filled with evil things.

This is how people find themselves in places that don't compliment who they are at their core. It starts as a thought, then followed by "steps" in the wrong direction. These "steps" may seem small, but the slightest deviation from a path can offset a person from arriving at their desired destination by a large distance, if the journey is long. So, **it would be wise to choose our path and steps carefully** (Matthew 7:13-14).

"Spiraling out of control" is a description of a specific situation when an airplane loses its ability to fully function and falls in a spiral-like pattern. The pattern can look like the pilot is doing it on purpose because it is consistent, but the fact of the matter is the plane is out of control. The plane is stuck in a loop that can destroy it and anything around it. Much like the pilot and the airplane, when a person is stuck in a spiritual downward spiral, it's difficult to tell whether they can or will regain control.

39 In-Plane Sight

Too often the early symptoms of a spiritual downward spiral are ignored. It is assumed that the poor choices are intentional and the "pilot" is in complete control of their direction and does not want to change. The assumption that the "spiraling" person has control can be based on misguidance, ignorance, and/or projections.

From observation and experience, people have the tendency to project when a situation makes them uncomfortable. "They knew what they were doing" is a phrase often used as an attempt to justify a hardened heart. As individuals we can't fix everything, but that doesn't mean we have to lack compassion. If we do not take the time to try to understand others, we cannot know a person's true status. Helping doesn't always require jumping in the plane, sometimes you can "radio the pilot" to check if they are spiraling on purpose or if they lost control and need help.

We all make choices. Some choices can be more obvious where they land in terms of being morally good or morally bad. More often than not, it is not clear how the "small" choices or changes to our space will affect us over time. When you see someone "spiraling" practice grace and withhold judgment. You don't know what they have been through or if they are "in control" or not. It should also be understood that everyone is capable of finding themselves in a compromised position.

A good thing is that God is not cruel, insecure, lazy, or incapable. He understands and can navigate any situation at any moment or length of time. **You do not have to change** in order for Him to help; **He loves you as you are** and will step in on your behalf (John 7:37-39). God can help you improve or recover from any situation or space.

Groups

People that have a sound mind try to be in places or create a space where things they deem as "good" can have access to them. But how easy is that in this world? It is difficult if not impossible because the world has gotten significantly smaller in the last 120+ years. Try to imagine 7 billion+ little atmospheres. Some of those spaces are going to come in contact with each other. Sometimes they blend, other times they repel. With the internet readily available to many, trends and cultures that can influence our spaces can spread worldwide overnight.

We established that living in the spirit and following God is the best-case scenario. But in our current world not everyone believes in the spiritual world, and not everyone follows God. In addition, people like to play the "what if" game to justify their selfish ambitions and project their mindset. Self-centeredness is very tempting to many and can be extremely difficult to detect by oneself. Cultures and trends that cultivate self-centeredness can skew the view of things that are generally understood to be "good" or "bad." This leaves people to create all kinds of spaces, including spaces that are confusing, corrupted, and/or evil.

When someone or something enters a space, things can get mingled. One atmosphere can inherit some of the things that the other has created, and vice versa. This occurrence can be observed at gatherings of all types. There are several terms for it: mob mentality, herd mentality, pack mentality, etc. Interestingly enough, many of the terms refer to the mental state of the group. The general study of what happens to people mentally when they gather is referred to as "Crowd Psychology." It's an interesting choice of words because crowds of people do not share one physical brain and it's unlikely that everyone in the group shares the same psychological profile.

These group "mental" situations can result in a variety of people behaving very similarly in a moment or over time. People that are sad can become happy. People that are not violent can become violent. People that are timid can become emboldened. People that are rational can become irrational. These are **observable revelations of the significance of shared spaces** (1 Corinthians 15:33). Sharing a space affects people physically, mentally, and spiritually.

Adults of a sound mind protect themselves mentally relatively well. Convincing an adult to change their mind or habits can be challenging over a long period of time, let alone in an instant. The resistance to change is strong enough to greatly oppose people they know and trust. A common experience of this mental defense manifests during family gatherings. People who share similar backgrounds, mindsets, and DNA can become significantly defensive against change when personal preferences are a topic of discussion.

So, how can strangers convince each other to feel and behave differently? In some instances there is no need for direct communication for a person to be influenced to act out of character. The phrase "caught up in the moment" describes when a person is persuaded to go against their better judgment and/or their developed character. It is a term often used when a person is describing actions they can't logically explain or justify.

Why is it that when we are "caught up in the moment" it feels like we are watching ourselves from the outside? Why do we feel somewhat out of control of our own bodies? Could it be that being "caught up in the moment" is a revelation of outside spirits having a direct influence on us? These experiences can happen with a crowd or an individual that has significant spiritual influence. A common term used for individuals with significant spiritual influence is "charisma."

These situations can be good or bad, it depends on the company you keep. **When there are two or three people together there is potential for shared spiritual experiences** (Matthew 18:20). At the end of the day, adults that have a sound mind are responsible for their choices. The direction where your mind is focused and the company you keep will have a significant influence on your earthly and spiritual space. That being said, **without God, those spaces or groups cannot be good** (1 John 2:15-17).

Know Your Role

As said previously, the functional structures on Earth reflect the structures and order of the spiritual world. Everything has a role, place, and level of authority. Everything is subject to the word of God. Whether you acknowledge it or not, there is someone or something that has authority over you. That authority can be physical, mental, emotional, professional, financial, spiritual, etc. It is important to understand that multiple things can have authority over you at the same time. This is how life can get messy.

As humans we cannot be masters of all. If we look at ourselves as a species (flesh and blood) and ignore that we are spiritual creatures, we become subjects (servants) of many things, including each other. If we allow ourselves to become subjects to a variety of things we will become self-destructive. This is because **an individual cannot serve more than one master** (Matthew 6:24). You also cannot be a competent master if you do not have complete authority. So, living solely as a flesh and blood being will have a person living in an endless cycle of division and confusion.

Let's look at the animal kingdom. From observation we can see that non-human creatures share some similar life experiences as we do while on Earth. They scavenge, hunt, multiply, protect, play, and maintain their lives to the best of their ability. Some move as a group and others as individuals.

The difference between the animal kingdom and humans is that creatures in the animal kingdom know their place. They know their role and what has authority over them. There is a clear structure that if left unprovoked by outside elements, the animal kingdom would maintain itself perpetually. This balance is possible because the other animals did not disobey God in the garden of Eden. Because they continue to be obedient to the will of God, **they are given all the provisions they need** (Luke 12:24). There is not a natural ecosystem on the planet that requires mankind's presence to survive. On the other hand, as much as mankind boasts about our abilities, we need these ecosystems for our survival.

To me it's clear, the system that is obedient to God (nature) has enough provisions to sustain life for itself and others abundantly. On the other side, the system that disobeys God (humans) has to rely on the abundance of the obedient system to sustain life. In addition, all the imbalance experienced in the obedient system can be linked directly or indirectly to the disobedient system's activity.

The experiences of death, famine, and violence in the animal kingdom can be an inherited experience from man's original sin, where the outcome is this fallen world. Since we were given dominion over the Earth and everything on it, it's likely that our choices affected the experiences of everything under our authority. To put it in a different frame, other creatures are like competent employees working under an underperforming manager. I believe these very observable examples should make us question our ability to function without divine guidance.

If you make the mistake of thinking humans have authority over the animal kingdom because of our abilities (physical or mental), just know that if ants decided to "play offense" against humans, we would be in very big trouble. That's just one type of insect. We as **humans have dominion over the living things on earth** because the authority has been given to us by God (Genesis 1:26). The authority we have as humans and the hierarchy the animal kingdom follows is a display of grace that gives us favor. It also provides insight on how we should follow God's instruction. Acknowledging our place and knowing the roles that God wants us to live out on Earth is the only way we can find balance.

Misguided Guidance

The reason why the Earth is currently in a "bad spot" in terms of the environment is because we (humans) are less than competent leaders when we rely on our own understanding and ability. We aren't as great as God, we aren't as loving as God, and we can't rule as well as God. We don't understand ourselves or have as much control over things like God does. That is because **we are** simply **an image of** what **God** is (Genesis 1:27).

We are made complete by having an intimate relationship with God, and sin causes separation between us and God. This separation from God as a species has led us to be unfit leaders and as a result we are destroying the things that give us life. **We have prioritized insignificant things over the significant**, all while thinking we are improving our lives when it detracts from it (James 5:1-6).

The things that we use money to get would be here regardless of money existing. The material things we create are the results of knowledge, inspiration, focus, and work; not money. Money should not be an incentive for living. When it is most useful, money is just a tool, not a purpose. Just like any tool, money can be misused, misunderstood, and mistaken as a solution to problems.

God is the God of finances too. Seek God's counsel in all things, including financial decisions. I understand that finances are deeply rooted into our world society, but we should not be subject to anything but God. In many instances money is being used as a destructive tool to distract people from discovering their true identity and seeking their God-given purpose. In other instances money is used to bridge gaps and distribute resources. Money isn't evil, worshiping money is.

Too often children's dreams and aspirations are smothered by deceived adults. There is a notion commonly fed and sometimes spoken directly to children, "That dream won't get you fed, you need a real job when you grow up." This is usually followed up with coercing the child towards a field that seems profitable at the time. **Teaching children to chase money over their interests is a** shortsighted and **unrighteous practice** (Ephesians 6:4).

Misguided Guidance

We all have different interests and abilities. The things we are interested in can be profitable regardless of what the current trend is. When I grew up, many of the children that played video games or rode skateboards were most likely told at some point to stop those activities and get a job. Fast forward to now, both of those activities are legitimate professions.

There is great value in seeing things through and following something that you are passionate about. In doing so you will most likely find a group of people that share the same passion as you. **Finding people that you can identify with and work with is a treasure all on its own** (Proverbs 27:17).

One of the things that corrupts us is the belief that we have to conform to the things that are "guaranteed" to get us money. That mentality narrows the playing field and creates unjustified competition. Often people are groomed to step on each other to get what they think they need. Too often people are willing to destroy another person for positions that are available elsewhere or for positions that can be created. The "whatever it takes" mentality will leave you throwing away the best parts of you for a title and pay that comes and goes like the wind.

Wealth is only useful if you're using it to do what you love, and many people mistake the love of their craft for the love of making money. Now **if you keep saying** you love money, **that will become your truth** at some point (Matthew 15:10-11). **The love of money is a path to destruction** (1 Timothy 6:10).

We all have gifts (James 1:16-18). It's important to know how to discern between what is fulfilling, and what is a "side effect" of using those gifts. For example, being a hustler is not restricted to a person that loves making money. I believe at every hustler's "core," there is a desire to make connections and/or be a part of a perceived improvement.

If money wasn't a factor, hustlers would still get fulfillment from connecting with people and being a part of an improvement. This is why people who have become successful in their "hustle" rarely stop. Often, they expand to other industries and/or offer help to people who share a similar mindset and are willing to learn. If money was their motivation, they probably would have stopped once they secured enough wealth to provide for several generations. So, "hustlers" can **find fulfillment in connecting with people and improving situations**; making money is a "side effect" of pursuing their core desire (1 Timothy 6:17-19).

Another misguided mindset/culture is the idolization of "winning." The "win at all costs" approach to life is a cancerous heart posture. More often than not, the people that "hate to lose" whether it be a game or a deal don't hate to lose, they hate feeling insecure. In those cases, "winning" has more value than money or anything else. In being a slave to pride, a person can be deceived to think that winning will heal past failures and/or solidify their "worthiness."

The posture of a **humble** loser **is greater than** that of a **prideful** winner (Proverbs 11:2). That truth becomes more obvious when interacting with a person who can be described as a "sore winner." Although they've won, their celebrations/presence can be repulsive. I believe this is due to a prideful spirit manifesting itself. Focusing all of your goals on "Winning" is willingly reducing your wonderfully-made being to a number. How much did you win? How many times have you won? What is your rank? In the end, souls will not be satisfied by these things.

Work & Play

Imagine being a part of a society where everyone had access to everything they felt they needed without having to work or pay for it. How likely would it be that you would use your free time to find or do the things you love to do? What's the likelihood that you would give away some of the things you've created or help complete?

Your first reaction might have been, "Why would I give stuff away?" My belief is that at some point you would have a surplus of whatever it is you do and won't feel the need to keep it for yourself. My prediction is at some point you would happily offer your service for free because of the absence of lacking. When you're of sound mind, it's easy to give when the fear of loss is not present.

How does that scenario make you feel in general? How do you think that scenario would play out for you? Is that an environment you would want for the people you care about?

If you had problems imagining and appreciating that "giving things away for free" scenario for a decent length of time, I wouldn't be surprised. The thoughts of "what other people would do" may have kept popping into your mind and ruined the moment. If it did, then you are consciously or subconsciously aware of the problem we all deal with: spiritual corruption.

It's spiritual because every person would have their needs filled in that situation. There would be no logical flesh and blood reason for anyone to want to disrupt that system. When people act contrary to the basic laws of nature like self-preservation or side with things that go against their own interests, there is most likely a strong spiritual influence on that person or group. Spiritual influence in general can be a good or bad thing, but we can have trouble appreciating that "good" scenario because consciously or subconsciously we know **mankind deals with tempting and corrupting spirits** (1 Corinthians 10:13).

Most people recognize that **the love of money** and power **corrupts** us as individuals and as a species (1 Timothy 6:10). We've seen throughout history what the love of those things can do to individuals and societies. It is also superficial. All the power in the world can't fill the void of feeling unloved, unappreciated, or unworthy.

The things of this world cannot give the spirit what it needs because the spirit is not of this world. Even if your initial motivation was to leave a legacy for your loved ones, the love of money and power always leaves a legacy of animosity, chaos, and destruction. That's the reason why we need to follow God. We do not have the capability to maintain order, peace, or anything truly good on our own.

When you live an unspiritual life and do not follow God, the work you do can be working against you. Fulfillment will always be fleeting no matter how many times you play it out. Earth should follow Heaven's lead, as we should follow God's. We can see this truth in our everyday lives. Jesus shared with us this wisdom in the form of a prayer. **Hallowed be thy name. Thy kingdom come. Thy will be done in Earth, as it is in Heaven.** (Matthew 6:9-10).

Chapter Reflection: In-Plane Sight

<u>Spaces</u>

❖ Can you think of a time when an environment you were exposed to influenced your lifestyle/habits for an extended amount of time? Example: Yes. I went to a concert, became an artist.

❖ How did you change your environment to reflect that different lifestyle/habit?

❖ Did that lifestyle affect your personal relationships? How?

❖ If possible, list milestones that display a cycle of influence in one area of your life. Example: Went to a concert. Listened more to music from that genre. Put artist's posters on the walls. Learned how to play an instrument. Became an artist. Joined a group of artists. Centered life around music.

Groups

- Have you ever been "caught up in the moment"? Was it when you were with a group or when you were with an individual?
- Do you think the outcome would have been better or worse if you didn't allow yourself to get "caught up in the moment"? Why?
- If your scenario from the questions above was "good," can you think of a "bad" situation and answer the same questions or vice versa if it was "bad"?

Know Your Role

- What are some things/people that have authority over you in your life?
- What are some things/people that you have authority over? Do you feel you do right by them?
- Do you think humans are balanced creatures compared to the rest of the animal kingdom? Why?
- Do you think humans cause a balance or imbalance to the natural world? Why?

Misguided Guidance

- Have you ever changed your aspirations or end goal because it didn't seem profitable? Do you think that was a wise decision?
- Has anyone ever tried to convince you to not do something you were passionate about? Why did you listen or not listen to them?
- Have you ever stopped somebody from pursuing something because you didn't think it was profitable? In hindsight, do you think that was fair to them?
- Have you ever traded your passion for a position? If so, what led to that?
- What do you think your gifts are? Do you feel like you're using them?
- Would you be willing to share your gifts without receiving any kind of pay or compensation?
- Are you willing to win at all costs? Why?

Work & Play

- Have you ever had a position where it was work but you enjoyed it? What was it? What did you like about it?

- When thinking about the utopian scenario described in this section of the book, do you think it would work? Why or why not?
- Would you wish limitless money and power for your circle of friends and family, or limitless love and appreciation? Why?

Chapter 3

<u>Our Voice</u>

The "sticks and stones" nursery rhyme is a lie. Words are one of the most significant things on earth, and they can certainly hurt people.

The things we say (written, verbally, or other) have the potential to last eternally. All living things on Earth will pass away at their appointed time, but words can go on. Written words can be spoken by others and spoken words can be written by others. Everyday communications can be remembered and re-lived potentially forever.

A simple earthly example of this is a quote from anyone who has passed away. The words they said are still here, but the person that said them is not. **We cannot fully comprehend the impact of our voice** (Proverbs 18:21). Words transcend dimensions and time which means they have some level of authority over this world.

Communication is the exchange of information. Basic human communication requires some level of self and situational awareness. To improve our ability to communicate we should seek guidance and calibration in those areas regularly. To be guided is to be led by something.

Calibration, in human context, is to assess and adjust mindsets and/or behaviors with the intent to reflect a set standard. In most cases guidance and calibration require external inputs. The types of inputs can include individuals, groups, and other beings. The best case scenario for us would be to be guided and calibrated by the Spirit of God, also known as the Holy Spirit. The Holy Spirit can work directly with you and through others to help guide and calibrate you.

Expression & Expectation

One reason human relationships are complicated is because everyone has their own way of expressing and receiving information. Because of this fact, we have to engage with others with the intent to understand. That is, if we desire healthy interactions. Many times internal definitions, methods of operation, experiences, and motivations cloud an individual's ability to truly listen to others and themselves.

Healthy communication is work. In my opinion healthy communication is listening for understanding and honest, considerate expression. I believe trying to understand someone is an act of love, and learning how you process and express yourself are practices of self-love.

It takes intent, humbleness, patience, community, and an unbreakable figurative mirror to learn healthy and honest expression of self. It takes all the things I just listed and a closed mouth to learn how to listen to others for understanding. From my observations, the priority of a relationship is revealed by the amount of effort one is willing to put into learning and communicating with the other in a healthy manner.

We cannot read the minds or hearts of men like God can, therefore it would be wise to pray for wisdom, clarity, presence, and love for all of your relationships, personal and other. After praying, opportunities will arise to apply the values you prayed for. You may not always respond in the way that you hoped for, but don't be discouraged. Character takes time to develop.

When it comes to our ability to communicate there is a stumbling block that is found at the feet of many, expectations. When we expect things, whether it be for a situation or from people, we are setting our perceived standards onto it and/or them. I say "perceived standards" because sometimes we set standards on other things, but do not always live by those standards. To hold a standard is to own the standard. If you don't live by the standard you're not holding or owning the standard, you are just observing the standard. Expectations are inspired by standards.

Having set standards that you live by can be beneficial, but projecting standards can be detrimental. To project standards is to project expectations. We have to conduct ourselves carefully when setting expectations on things, situations, and people. We have to acknowledge the fact that our expectations are always personal and may not be in alignment with the standards of everything or everyone involved. Without taking great care when considering the situation, we may set some unreasonable and unhealthy expectations.

When it comes to expectations it helps to communicate them clearly and as soon as possible. That doesn't mean telling someone your marriage expectations on the first date, it means you shouldn't assume people know or hold your expectations. Occasionally expressing your satisfactions and disappointments with people you engage with can improve that relationship; even if it is a seasoned relationship.

Can a person choose to live by standards not created by them? Absolutely. I choose to live by the standards that God has given me through the Bible and the Holy Spirit. Does that mean I can or should place those standards on everyone I come into contact with? No. To enforce a personal preference or standard onto a scenario or people is to take an authoritative role. We must be humble enough to acknowledge situations where we may not be entitled to that authority. Assuming authority is not something I would recommend.

With a clearer theoretical understanding of expectations, I will share some of my experience in regard to calibrating expectations.

In general, I try to calibrate my expectations to "expect God" and nothing else. I have experienced that when I only apply my human standards and expectations to a person or situation, I set myself up with my own foolishness. But if I place all of my expectations in Him, I can walk in confidence knowing that I've submitted myself to His will. Does that mean I just sit and wait for "magic" to happen? No. My relationship with God has taught me that when I give Him everything, He returns identity, purpose, responsibilities, instructions, and provisions to carry out His will. His will is very good.

As I move through the world, I expect God's will to be done. What that means is the only thing I can truly rely on is God showing up in some way. My experience has led me to plan and operate to the best of my ability and be prepared for things to look different than I expected. In doing so the potential of having negative emotional responses like disappointment or anger is lowered.

I have noticed that I don't get overwhelmed by emotions when I choose to fix my thoughts on God's character and promises. That choice allows me to see the situation clearer, and many times this clarity has enabled me to be more flexible and optimistic about situations. I believe the experience of outcomes looking different than anticipated is a part of the observable truth of God's holiness. He is truly different. Unless He gives us a vision, we can't see what He sees.

As a believer in Christ I expect other believers to behave in a way that aligns with the principles and standards set in the Bible. Does that mean I have the authority to just walk into any church and start criticizing? No. As a follower of Christ I have to recognize that believers are (or should be) submitted to God, not me. If I'm just busting through doors I have no idea what kind of progressions or regressions that church has experienced.

To calibrate my expectations for an unfamiliar person or church, I have to take the time to build a relationship with them. If I am to share my observations or constructive criticisms with individuals or groups, I earnestly seek to be led by the Holy Spirit. Who expresses correction with grace, love, and conviction.

As a husband and father I expect me, my wife, and our children to behave in a way that aligns with the biblical and personal standards set for our household by the Bible, the Holy Spirit, me, and my wife. As the head of the household I have to live by the standards and expectations that are set. God makes it very clear in scripture that He does not like hypocrites, so I try my best not to be one. Yes, in the last sentence I gave myself a disclaimer by saying "I try my best." That is me admitting that I'm not perfect and I can only live by the grace of God. It is not an excuse, it's the truth.

I wish I could be the perfect example for my family, but I am not. When I fall short of His standard, I humble myself before God by repenting and asking for direction. I ask Him to name my shortcomings and how I can reconcile with Him and my family. So, I calibrate my expectations as the leader of my family by looking at how my Heavenly Father leads me. My prayer is that I always meet my family with grace, love, and conviction.

One of the most damaging mindsets in terms of expectation is the expectation of perfection. There can be a variety of reasons that cause this mindset. Though a person may not be responsible for what caused them to expect perfection, they are responsible for their decisions.

We are all imperfect and inconsistent. To expect perfection or perpetual consistency from anyone on this Earth is setting the relationship up for disappointment and/or failure. Setting your expectation of what you perceive as perfection will also harden your heart to the concept of grace. Everyone who has ever and will ever live, has lived by God's grace. If we were spared by grace, we should seek to live by grace.

The only one that loves you perfectly is Jesus; everyone else will fall short.

It is healthy to express opinions, set standards, and to work towards self improvement. Life becomes shaky when our convictions become condemnation for others, and our hearts are harder than the foundation we stand on. My suggestion to anyone who struggles with being critical or sees themselves as a perfectionist is to ask the Holy Spirit to guide you in getting counsel (spiritual and clinical). Good counsel will help you navigate expectations, subdue perfectionist mindsets, and improve the relationships in your life.

Wakes to Waves

Things said affect other people, which means spiritual spaces are affected by words. I have no doubt that if you're reading this you've experienced the power that words can have, good or bad. A word can encourage for a lifetime; a word can leave a heart broken for a lifetime. That is because

words can usher life or death into someone's spirit (Proverbs 15:4).

The power of words is something that is not respected enough. We throw them around with very little regard to the wakes they make. We pretend that they are easily wiped clean like water on a glass, when in fact they can be more powerful than time and matter.

When we speak there is potential for things to change. If someone with authority says "do this," and it is done, the history of the world can be changed from their words. When you read "someone with authority," you may have envisioned a person holding what is considered to be a "high title" in our society, but we all can be in a position of authority.

Being a parent, sibling, friend, lover, teacher, manager, and consultant are all positions of authority because we give those positions or titles some level of authority over our lives at some point. All those positions and titles are our neighbors and we theirs. This is why we are told to love our neighbors. Since it is impossible for us to know how our behavior may impact other people, we should be intentionally trying to approach everyone with love. When you come from a place of love, your words and gestures can have God in them because **God is love** (1 John 4:8).

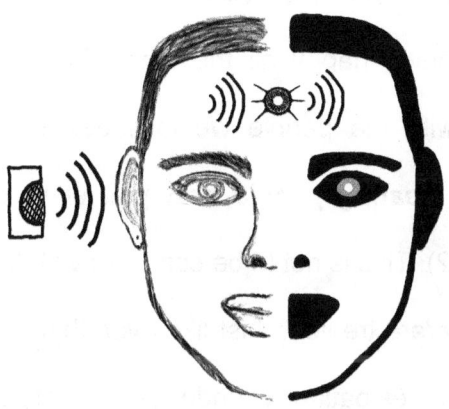

Messages in the physical world are received mentally & spiritually

Influence from the spiritual world can dictate earthly behavior

Love Who?

So, what does "loving thy neighbor" look like in this world? I can tell you what it's not. It's not everyone holding hands and being happy all the time. That's not even our experience with the people we love deeply. **Loving your neighbor is treating people how you want to be treated** (Luke 6:31-32). This is not to be confused with treating people how you were/are treated. Just like everything else in life that is good, love takes patience, kindness, maturity, and effort.

In living amongst others we are bound to interact with people that may not compliment our personalities. Not having compatible personalities does not mean we have to be at each other's throat. We can learn to love and respect people that may seem offensive or incompatible. To learn how to do this we need a standard to live by, a feedback system that guides toward the set standard, the energy to work, and the willingness to work. I believe the only possible way to truly love someone, familiar or stranger, is to have the spirit of truth and love live inside of you. That spirit is the Holy Spirit.

Are there practical ways to exercise loving other people? absolutely. As much as things are rooted in spirituality, we can seek understanding for how to receive and express love effectively.

Personal experiences, academic education, and professional counseling can help us gain the knowledge of communication. These can be helpful instruments for most relationships. What I've experienced is that when we engage in exercises without being led and empowered by the Holy Spirit, we become discouraged and depleted. In being human we have a fixed capacity. Exercising without getting renewed and replenished will lead to injury.

Let's take a step back and ponder the possibility of being the recipient of love from a stranger. Imagine moving into a new neighborhood and one neighbor approached you consistently with kindness. Not cartoonishly kind, not looking to gossip, they just seem available and kind hearted. I believe that with enough time you would develop some level of appreciation for that person. Now if you were to reciprocate kindness consistently, there is a high probability that a bond would be created. The bond may not become deep, but at the very least, a mutual level of respect will be shared.

Why does this mutual respect of persons matter? Because it is impossible to love someone as yourself when you don't equate their humanness to yours. Not seeing people as people makes it difficult to "meet people where they are." It's tempting to summarize people as their flaws because it feeds a sinful desire to be "better" than others. Pride is ugly. When there is a mutual level of respect between parties the potential for sharp negative reactions during conflict decreases while the capacity to listen increases.

Let's return to the kind neighbor scenario. With time passing it is possible that you may notice a habit or characteristic of that neighbor that doesn't perfectly align with your preferences. But because you have been exposed to their kindness and shared yours, you will most likely consider ways to resolve the conflicting issue instead of summarizing them as an issue. Genuine appreciation of persons increases the durability of relationships.

At the end of the day, loving a neighbor doesn't require every single aspect of love to be balled together and operate at a high level. Loving a neighbor is accepting the fact that they are an imperfect person just like you. Not focusing on "imperfections," but rather sharing grace and desiring to live in peace.

When it comes to navigating people that seem to make an effort to *not* get along with you, keep your peace. **Returning negativity** because "that's what they did" **puts you in a worse space** (Proverbs 10:12). The time and energy you put into retaliation is time and effort you could have spent on things that deserve your time. This does not mean we let people walk all over us. Returning negativity and administering consequences are not the same.

We should try our best to approach everyone from a place of love and respect. If someone is out of line, try to approach the situation with grace and mercy. Grace is giving something that is not earned, and mercy is withholding a justified punishment. Oftentimes when these are exercised, an opportunity for the offense to be corrected presents itself.

Yes, they may say and do things that trigger an emotional reaction, but you may be surprised at how effective being slow to anger is with maintaining internal peace, and diffusing external conflicts. In exercising patience accompanied with the Holy Spirit, you will find peace beyond understanding and become unbothered by many situations that would warrant "retaliation" in a flesh and blood mindset.

Practice praying for the people who you don't get along with. If someone comes at you from a place of anger don't look to multiply their anger or open the door for yours. It is more possible to recognize and reconcile wrong doings when anger is subdued. You can't find peace if both parties are feeding from the same unclean spirits. The charge of loving your neighbor may be good for your neighbor, but it's essential for you. It reduces the possibility of getting caught in the crossfire of spirits that mean to defile you.

Many of the charges in the Bible are written for our personal benefit. **They are written so we can enjoy life as much as possible** (Matthew 6:31-33). When we are charitable, helpful, slow to anger, encouraging, and empathetic, our quality of life is increased. When you give, do not worry about what the receiver will do next. Whether it's your time, money, or materials, having the ability to give is something to be grateful for. Do the deed and be on your way.

In some way, shape, or form we are all neighbors. So our "neighbor" is literally everyone in the world. Appreciating similarities, respecting differences, and well-wishing are all easier conditions to live in than division, malice, and war. Treating people how you want to be treated is a part of the blueprint for internal and external peace.

Love Is...

When it comes to words that are supposed to describe human experiences it is wise to learn the academic definitions and compare them to observable or practiced experiences. I believe many problems relating to our understanding of love stem from adopting popular culture's "definitions" of love. "Definitions" is in quotes because ideas and beliefs expressed in popular culture (pop culture) seem to be interpretations of ideas and beliefs from something else. Because ideas and beliefs expressed through pop culture are more likely to be interpretations, it is virtually impossible to set clear definitions and boundaries.

This is why pop culture is so popular. As spiritually fallen creatures, the practice of defining things according to our personal standard is tempting. This is a temptation that every human finds appealing in one way or the other, hence why it's popular. A part of the temptation that led to original sin was the temptation to be like God. God is *the* definer. So looking to become the definer is looking to become your own god.

From my observations, it seems that pop culture has reduced love to emotional states or biological responses. Emotions can be a part of love. Biological chemistry can be a part of love. But if you look at what many consider acts of true love you will see that love is not fully dependent on emotions or chemicals. From my experiences, studies, and observations, love is proven by how it is lived out more than how it is felt. In my opinion, it's only love if you are willing to "walk the walk."

For instance, I love my family, but that doesn't mean we don't bump heads. It means although we bump heads, I am still willing to love them. The "willing" part is so important in understanding love. To be willing is to be *and* do. Which means when we love, we should be willing to be selfless, willing to be patient, willing to communicate in truth, willing to be kind, willing to work towards goals, willing to listen, etc. None of those need to align with how we feel at the moment to execute them. They also do not require a relationship with the receiving person in order for us to perform them.

My personal experiences include me thinking or communicating to the person "I must love you because I'm sharing my... (insert favorite food, or something personally valuable)." There are also situations where I'm willing to go "above and beyond" with no expectation or desire for a return.

In my opinion, thoughtful actions at times when we don't feel like doing them are clearer indicators that true love is present. I do not believe I am alone in considering those instances as indicators of true love. Some of the most touching stories, fiction and nonfiction, are the stories where a person exhibits love when the situation is not conducive to warm feelings or happy endings.

It's also important to understand that it is nice when that willingness goes both ways, but perfect balance is not always going to be the experience. Love is knowing that you may be carrying the "weight" of the relationship at times and be willing to do just that. Love is also the practice of wishing someone the best although it may not be reciprocated.

To be clear, you can wish someone well from a distance. You can love someone, from a distance. Staying in a relationship where the expressed love is consistently one-sided can be harmful mentally, spiritually, and sometimes physically. In these unhealthy situations, love yourself enough to love from a distance.

Idolization, confusion, desperation, and lust can manipulate our emotions to make us think we are in a loving situation when we are not. That is why reducing love to an internal feeling is very problematic. Emotions alone do not have the consistency, durability, or strength to convey or maintain love how God defines it. God-centered love inspires action and should not produce feelings of emptiness, anxiety, or fear. If love is present, there should be **observable evidence that love is present** (1 Corinthians 13:4-8).

Being in love is work, a lot of work. You can feel like you love somebody to death, but if you don't **invest time and energy into** that **love**, your access to that love will change (1 Peter 4:8). Notice I did not say that love will die. Love does not die; it is a fruit of the Spirit of God. It can change, but it does not die. When we abandon the spirit via inaction, it feels like it's gone, but it is not. This is how we can love or wish well for people who are no longer active in our lives.

When we hear "love is everlasting," sometimes we like to romanticize it, but we really can't fully comprehend the reality of everlasting. Everlasting love sounds great when the love is reciprocated, but what about when it's not? It can be devastating. Yes, you were in love, but if that love is not or cannot be maintained by both parties, that love will change.

Habitual, mental, and emotional adjustments have to be made in order to remain a healthy individual. Love is a living thing. Living things on Earth have seasons. Don't romanticize a season; live in the now. Romanticizing a season will leave you stuck in the past and/or experiencing resentment. Being present can teach you how to love differently and appreciate the changes instead of rejecting them. The love of today should be prioritized over the love from yesterday.

Loving something does not mean you will always have access to that something in the form you are familiar with. Loving something does not mean it is obligated to love you back. Loving something does not mean you will automatically love it the way it wants or deserves to be loved. Love is not subject to time, money, gestures, titles, or words. This is true not just in romantic relationships, but with family and friends as well. Love should not be expecting or held for ransom.

One of the hardest things to emotionally process while growing into and through adulthood, is growing apart. Sometimes people view growing apart as a negative experience because what was good, no longer seems good. The truth is, what may seem bad to you, may not be bad for someone else. People who were your friends "back then," does not mean they are not your friends now because you don't spend the same time or do the same things with them. A family is not broken because they no longer live under the same roof. Out of sight does not always mean out of mind.

Sometimes our journeys require separation. Some plants can be bunched together while others need their space. We should encourage the people we love to grow into their own being. Projecting who a person was to you onto who they are currently, is not loving or respectful to that person. This can in-turn cause more damage than good in that relationship. Try to recognize people for who they are *today*, not who you think they were or should be, and move accordingly.

Situations change, people change. Our core character may not change, but our habits, interests, and perspectives certainly can. Considering these changes, communication is necessary for that relationship to remain healthy. A significant amount of time may pass, but in most cases it is better to start an awkward conversation as opposed to never speaking to them again.

Bring your love "up to speed." Even if there is conflict in the relationship, don't let that conflict keep your mind in the past. Reflect on why you are hurt or on "bad terms," and pray to learn forgiveness and peace. Sometimes stating, "I cherished our friendship for what it was. I know we don't get along now, but I hope you are well wherever you are." is what is necessary for a relationship to move forward.

The Bible explains the fundamentals of what love is in the letter Paul wrote to the Corinthians, and Jesus' life on Earth was the perfect example of living in love on Earth. The reality is, God is love; which means only He can define it. When we try to redefine love according to our personal desires things become unclear, confusing, and skewed.

Taking on human notions of love can lead you in the wrong direction. We are born into this world only knowing our caregivers at birth and their perceptions of love. It is important to acknowledge that it is a blessing to be born into a truly loving environment. Many have not been afforded the luxury of experiencing love as God defines it as a child. So, as adults we should audit our habits and definitions with the Bible as our frame of reference. This includes how we define and impart love.

Love Unlimited

Many try to convince themselves and others that we only have a fixed amount of love within us, but that is not the truth. Our love is only limited by our willingness to give it. **If you're willing to give true love, God will supply it** (John 15:9-12). In terms of our "supply" of love, my belief is that we are born with a portion of love according to God's grace. I believe the choices we make throughout life determine whether that portion is increased or depleted.

According to scripture, **love is the highest priority** when it comes to serving the Lord (Matthew 22:36-40, 1 Corinthians 13:1-3). God is The Provider. He supplies everything we need to serve Him. If a person is looking to truly serve God, they should know that they will have access to an unlimited supply of love. Understand this, access is only useful when it is used. We must turn to Him and submit to His will. If we truly seek to be a vessel of God, His love should flow through us.

A practical example of how our love is not limited can be seen in childhood development. As we grow, we meet more people. We can get to know them as family and/or friends. From these developed relationships, we may learn to love a significant amount of people at a fairly young age (parents, siblings, extended family, childhood friends, etc.). Experiencing this variety of love for different people tells me that love is bountiful and person-specific.

If a person has the capability to love individual members of family and friends at the same time, where does the idea of limitations come from? Does a person have to stop loving their brother in order to love their friend? No. Is there a specified number of people that I can care about? No. With time a person can learn to love many people in many different ways. And just when you think you can't love any more, a baby can reveal a larger capacity for love.

Understanding the context in which one can love makes it possible to love more and not become depleted or overzealous. Love is unlimited because God is infinite. He is willing to supply love if we are willing to share it. That being said, the Bible instructs us to **be good stewards of what we are given** (Matthew 25:29).

Love is something we can steward. Being a good steward is to manage something well. To manage something well you have to understand your strengths and weaknesses in regard to what you are managing. Prayer, counsel, and self-reflection help us calibrate to the season of life we are in. For these tools of calibration to be effective we may have to release some precepts that are deeply rooted.

I do not believe there is only one person in the world that has the potential to be your best friend, significant other, or "soulmate." Technically, the term soulmate is not biblical. It may be derived from the mystery of two becoming one, but that is a mystery that is restricted between husband and wife. The term is problematic in my opinion because it can imply that one person's existence and purpose is dependent on another's. I believe this is erroneous thinking and may restrict your willingness to love. God is the only being that completes our souls. Without a relationship with Him we are truly dead and there is no meaning for life.

 I believe His love and grace is manifested through others, and He joins people that compliment each other. My belief is that those roles can last a season or a lifetime. I would be cautious to receive a mentality that could put me in a position to feel like life is incomplete or meaningless without the other person(s). Now that doesn't mean you should live in isolation or go around ending friendships and breaking hearts. It means cherish the love(s) you have. Know that if you're still breathing, God has a purpose for you. Acknowledge that the willingness to love, love again, or not love is your choice.

 Love is a gift that is rooted in spirituality and experienced in this reality. A strong physical manifestation of love is experienced when we weep. Weeping comes in times of great pleasure and pain. We weep when our physical bodies cannot process emotions in their more raw, spiritual form. The body defaults to tears, sound, and sometimes the inability to stand or move. It is important to understand that pain needs to be processed, not just put away. Pleasure should be enjoyed, but not idolized.

Love is an everlasting experience that requires the infinite wisdom of God to navigate safely. God blesses us with as much love as we can handle. As humans we only "scratch the surface" in our experiences of love and **we cannot comprehend how much God loves us** (Ephesians 3:17-19).

True or False

God is truth. He is truth in the sense of being all knowing and honest, but it should be understood that **He is literally truth** (John 14:6). When you seek the truth, you are seeking God. When you hear and speak truth, the words have God in them. Confirmation words like "yes", "I am", "it is" and variations of those things are spiritually significant. That is why we are charged to speak and live in truth. When we do not, we take a position that is hostile towards the Spirit of God and open ourselves to unclean spirits. **In the absence of God there can only be darkness and evil** (1 John 1:5).

This is why the act of asking questions is spiritually significant. Seeking knowledge and understanding are acts that can invite God into a situation. That is why when we ask questions diligently, we will find the answer. **God is not withholding to those that seek answers** (Matthew 7:7-8).

This is a revelation of His fairness and grace. When we consciously choose to not seek understanding or truth, we open ourselves to spirits of deception and confusion. To be clear, it's one thing to be oblivious or uneducated; it's another to be willfully ignorant.

Avoiding opportunities to learn are missed opportunities to have God guide our lives. **God is willing to teach and guide** (John 16:13-15). There is no topic off limits or detail too small to inquire about. Open your heart and mind to ask and listen for everything you wonder. The journey of recognizing the truth often requires us to learn tangential truths about the subject in question. Without context or significant knowledge of the subject and surrounding subjects, we would not be able to recognize truth.

The more you seek Him, the more familiar you will get with His character and His "voice." That being said, you have to acknowledge and receive Him in order to get to know Him. Like any relationship, knowing a person's character and voice takes time and interaction. So when you ask God questions, don't assume the first thing you think or the first person you get an answer from is His answer. Diligently look for the truth and you will find it.

If you get an answer that is not the truth, it will be revealed. At that point **it is up to you to keep searching** until it is done (Jeremiah 29:11-14). Even if someone unintentionally or intentionally gives a false report, **that issue can be corrected** if finding the truth is the goal (James 5:19-20). Therefore, we should always be seeking the truth, even if we think we know what the truth is. Doing so is seeking God and following that path will always bring life to your soul.

So now that we understand what truth is. Where it comes from. And the benefits of speaking and living in truth. What does it mean to speak false statements or live falsely?

False things can distract, divert, and unhinge you from finding truth. False thinking leads to miscommunication, misleading, and withholding. False thinking creeps in and takes you away from God a small step at a time. This is why we need a close relationship with the Spirit of Truth. Things that are false can be very deceiving because they usually cater to our carnal desires. **The flesh tries its best to justify greed, lust, idolatry, envy, and other unclean things** with the help of falsehoods (Galatians 5:19-21).

This is why phrases like "fake it till you make it" are popular in superficial circles. It's a trap! Falsehoods built on falsehoods make it more difficult to recognize truth. As a result, the person is surrounded by lies. The "fake it" becomes the only reality that person knows, and who that person was is somewhere lost within them.

To be clear, in most cases there is nothing wrong with trying something new or learning by trial and error. If that's the situation, step into the role of being a student and humble yourself. Honest work will yield honest rewards. **Beware of circles that encourage falsehoods and pretentiousness** in exchange for anything (2 Timothy 2:15-16). My encouragement is to try your best to be as authentic as possible in every situation. Let God order your steps and don't let fear dictate how you move.

Our flesh betrays us because it is unrighteous. **We are born into sin**, which includes lies (Romans 5:12). Many people are taught early in life to avoid the truth in order to avoid things that are considered negative repercussions. This teaching is why consistently speaking and hearing the truth is such an unfamiliar and uncomfortable practice in many spaces.

The widespread disregard of truth in exchange for comfort has molded many communities into houses of cards. Being in an untruthful environment can create an atmosphere of confusion strong enough to where people will believe their own lie. Unfortunately people use religion as a tool to obtain or maintain worldly statuses. Religious practices without spiritual understanding creates spiritually numb people. When the people don't have a relationship with the Spirit of Truth they are more susceptible to deception.

Because our sinful nature has a fear of truth, a fear of being uncovered. **We feel the shame similar to what Adam and Eve felt when** their eyes were opened, and **their truth was revealed** (Genesis 3:8-10). The shame from the revelation of truth will never be as bad as the shame from hidden lies being revealed unwillingly. All things hidden will be revealed, so maintaining a lie is just compounding the offense.

Have you ever made the decision to tell the truth despite the fear of the possible consequences? It's actually freeing to a degree. Even if the result is something that seems unfavorable, **there is a weight lifted** that no lie could hold (John 8:31-32). I believe this is something that many people have experienced. You get that liberating feeling when you choose to be truthful because you are practicing a godly principle. It doesn't matter who you are or what you believe in. He is very generous and rewards good practices.

Following a Godly principle doesn't mean you have an active relationship with God; it means you will experience His grace in that area of your life. If you have experienced the relief of being truthful, try to imagine having His grace in all areas of your life. It is possible if you seek Him. Receiving His grace never gets old.

God loves us all and patiently waits to be with us. He's like a parent with a small child who is learning how to walk. He stands close with His arms out. He'll let you try to step on your own and **He's there to guide and catch you if you misstep** (Psalms 37:23-24). The thing is, if you choose to avoid His hands, you can't get mad at Him when you fall. Admitting you need help opens opportunities to see how God can keep you from hurting yourself.

A part of living in truth is taking responsibility for actions. Acknowledging our role in things that happen is very important for our mental, emotional, and spiritual health. Living in truth is not always pretty and the consequences of our actions can be a heavy burden to carry alone. This is why we are told to confess our sins to Jesus. Our sins are a part of our truth. **Confessing them to Jesus allows us to be forgiven of them and relieves us from holding everything in** (Matthew 11:28-30).

God can give the peace, clarity, and courage to endure situations where the truth hurts. Take the time to self-reflect, humble yourself, and exchange the false comfort that comes with lies. Receive the peace that surpasses all understanding. Seek to understand and apply values that help you grow and live with the Spirit of Truth.

Looking back at all the things we can do with our voice, what do you think our Father in Heaven can do with His? Consider the fact that words can transcend time, change the course of history, and spark creation. We can conclude that our words have the ability to operate on a level greater than Earth and time. Consider that the beginning of our **existence began with the Word of God** (Genesis 1:3). Please take thought on how you use your voice.

Chapter Reflection: Our Voice

Intro

- What's a word that has stuck with you your whole life? How has it impacted you?
- Have you considered that everything you say has the potential to have a lasting effect on your life and/or other people's lives?

Expression & Expectation

- Have you ever compared and contrasted your personal definitions of words and phrases with the definitions found in dictionaries? The Bible? Why or why not?
- In a discussion where something seems unclear, do you ask for clarity or continue the conversation?
- Considering your "average" day, do you think you express yourself more honestly or less honestly? Why?
- Do you live by the standards you expect?

- Do you think it is difficult to live by your standard? If so, what is the hardest part?
- If you could summarize all of your standards in a short sentence, what would that sentence be?
- How do you express your expectations and how frequently do you express them?
- Do the people around you express their expectations directly to you?
- Have you ever had to let go of your expectations? Why? How did you experience that emotionally?

Wakes to waves

- Has there been a situation where you said something that was thought to be insignificant but ended up having a larger impact than what you anticipated? What was it?

Love Who?

- In reflecting on this section, what is something that spoke to you but you find difficult to practice? Why do you think it's difficult for you?

Love is...

- In your relationships, do you assume a person knows exactly what you want or do you clearly communicate it?
- Do you think you deserve everything you ask for? Why or why not?
- Do you give everyone what they ask for? Why or why not?
- Do you think love requires compromising? Why or why not?
- In your relationships, what do you value more - gestures or willingness?
- After reading this section, what is your definition of love?

Love Unlimited

- Do you think your love is limited? Why?
- Do you think there is a general way to love, or do you think it is person specific?
- How can you express love to a stranger? A neighbor? A friend?

True or False

- Have you ever avoided the truth? Why? In hindsight, do you think avoiding the truth yielded a good end result?
- List some things you have accepted as truth.
- Have you accepted them as truth because they were given to you as truth, or have you reflected on those things and believe that they are true?
- What are some things you believed were true that you realized were not?
- What are some things you do to seek the truth?
- What are some obstacles that hinder finding the truth?
- Have you ever been stuck in a lie that as time went on, you had to lie more to uphold the lie? What was the experience? In hindsight, do you think it would have been easier to have told the truth?
- Have you ever felt you had to "fake it till you made it"? Did you make it? If you made it, by whose definition?
- Of all the circles you are involved in, how many of them value integrity and honesty?

❖ Have you ever made the decision to tell the truth despite the fear of the possible consequences? How did you feel after?

Chapter 4

<u>The Void</u>

From being born of this world, mankind is born with a void (John 3:6-7). There is a place within us that is empty, lacking, and unfilled. This void exists because of original sin. Sin is a word for actions that cause separation between us and God. God is Holy and Sovereign. When we violate His set standards it goes against His holy and sovereign "nature," and in a sense, we get repelled from His presence.

We were designed as spiritual beings to live in the fullness that comes with God's presence. When Adam decided to be disobedient and eat from the tree of knowledge of good and evil, **he decided to exchange the knowledge and awareness of his spirit for the knowledge and awareness of his flesh** (Genesis 3:6-7). From that decision we (all of mankind) inherited separation from our creator and a portion of spiritual ignorance. Sin is the root cause for the experience of living with a void.

In being separated from His spirit, we lost a great amount of perspective. Living in the spirit is a state of life that is much greater than what we know. The flesh that we are familiar with is not worthy of being in God's presence. This is why when we die our flesh is returned to dust and we stand before God in our spiritual body on the day of judgment.

Fertile Ground

I've heard this question quite often, "Why would God not want man to have knowledge?" It's not that he did not want man to have knowledge in general, the forbidden fruit was from **the tree of knowledge of good and evil** (Genesis 2:17). God knows what men were designed for and knew that the knowledge of good and evil would corrupt us. God created provisions for man so that we could live in the spirit and have direct communication with Him. In knowing and having a close relationship with God, who is good, there would be no benefit for man to know evil.

A small child does not need to know the atrocities of this world. The only thing a small child needs to know is the love, care, guidance, and protection it receives from its caregivers. As a child gets older and more mature, awareness, comprehension, and ability to navigate the world will increase. That is why God instructs us to be like children. Not children in terms of immature thoughts and behavior, but in submission and obedience to our heavenly Father for all things. Doing so will help us navigate life.

The more time we spend with Him, the more mature we become. Maturity is not the ability to "stand" on your own. Maturity is knowing and understanding your identity, then living true to that identity. God created us and knows our true identity. When we grow in our spiritual maturity, we become more complete as a being. We become more like the being God designed us to be.

So, the next question one could ask is, "Why would God put the tree of knowledge of good and evil in the garden of Eden and give it fruit if the fruit was forbidden?" The garden of Eden was a special garden that was given to Adam to oversee. This tells me that there is something significant about the things planted in the garden. **The tree of life is also within the garden** (Genesis 2:9). Adam's responsibility to keep it may be connected to mankind's responsibility to maintain dominion over the Earth.

I believe it's possible that the things planted in the garden establish what we know as "nature" on Earth. These can include things that establish the earthly laws of physics, the seasons of life, the truth (the reality) of good and bad things, and more. So, the tree of knowledge of good and evil most likely had to be there; that's probably why God put it there.

The tree yields fruit because everything in the garden is good and everything in it bears "fruit" in one way or another. It is important to consider that what is bad for one can be good or suitable for another. The tree being there was not an attempt to tempt mankind. I believe it is a requirement for life on Earth. **God does not tempt; evil things tempt us, and it is up to us to make a choice** (James 1:13-14).

We have the choice to be obedient or give into temptation; this is the reality of free will. We do not know what the results would have been if Adam and Eve successfully resisted temptation. It's possible that in being obedient, the serpent would have been exposed and removed from the garden. It's possible that we would have been given the ability to digest the knowledge of good and evil at some point, but what's done is done. **God still gives us provisions** and a choice to be with Him, so all is not lost (II Corinthians 12:9).

The Search

Living with a void is mentally, emotionally, and physically draining. It creates a cycle of seeking satisfaction by the flesh, soul, and spirit. These things are motivated to find what is missing, but aren't fully equipped to recognize and fulfill the missing component.

Our flesh is content with what is on Earth because it is of the earth, but the rest of our being senses there is more. One of the seasons where many people feel the void is when transitioning into adulthood. Many people develop a desire or hunger to find purpose in that season of life. We are compelled to ask, "What's it all for?" in our maturing minds and bodies. In becoming adults **it is revealed that there is more than what we knew as children** (I Corinthians 13:9-12).

Through our limited understanding we do many things to try to fill that void and answer that question. Naturally, many people focus on works of the flesh because that is the reality we are born into. In addition, many societies have been consciously undermining spirituality. Without looking to the Spirit for answers concerning the spirit, the search to fill the void will be fruitless. It will be fruitless in the sense that the things you try to fill the void with will not satisfy the desire to be complete. The actions or achievements during that time may satisfy your flesh and blood for a moment, but that satisfaction, if any, is short lived. **There is not a success in the world that can fill a spiritual void** (Mark 8:36-37).

So how does one start "the search"? Good news - God is literally everywhere. You can, with faith, ask God right now, "God, how do I fill this void?" And God will begin to reveal to you the work He has done for you. Read that again. God has already done the work that will give you everything you need and more. **God has had you on His mind before there was life on Earth** (Ephesians 1:4). When you call on Him it's like asking Him to "pull back the curtain." The provisions are already there, you just haven't been able to perceive or receive them.

It's important to understand that the provisions "behind the curtain" are not just tangible things. God has provisions for intangible things like mental health and heart posture transformation as well. It's important to know that all the tangible and intangible earthly things are not the prize and should not be our goal. Having an intimate relationship with God is the true prize. God has provisions for you to be in an intimate relationship with Him. There is nothing that you can present or need from God that will surprise or overwhelm Him. He is present and loving. There is nothing greater than being close to Him.

While God knows everything about us, we cannot know everything about Him. So, it is imperative that we do not project our thoughts, abilities, and limitations onto God. He is beyond anything we can fathom. Everything He does is different. His responses are not like our responses. His patience is not like our patience. His faithfulness is not like our faithfulness. He does not sit around and wait to be called to start and/or finish working like we do. He knows all possible outcomes and has planned, created, and dressed everything for every possibility.

That is why when we follow His lead, the path is good and **the burden is light** (Matthew 11:28-30). If there were something to always ask God for, it would be for His will to be done in you and your life. That is my suggestion.

The Void

Follow Freely

It is human nature to follow and/or be submitted to something. We do not have the capability to be truly independent. We were created to follow God, and He has given us free will because love is a choice. This means when we don't follow God, we will follow something else. That something will be inferior to Him.

This is why God refers to humans as sheep in the Bible. Sheep are herd animals that are not known for being clever or independent survivalists. Sheep that stray away from the herd and/or shepherd, can find themselves in compromising situations because of their limited abilities. When they have a good shepherd leading and protecting them, they receive provisions and security that are beyond their ability to produce.

We are all born unrighteous because of original sin. So in that unrighteous state, think of us as sheep in the wild. There is a natural tendency to just do what everyone else is doing with the hope of heading in a decent direction. When a person submits themselves to God, God refers to them as

"His sheep," which is an important distinction from being "a sheep."

Having a good shepherd is the ideal situation because of the reasons described earlier. **People who** choose to follow other things and **rebel against God are** described as **vicious wolves** and other predatory animals throughout biblical scripture (Acts 20:28-29). Being described as a predatory creature when **the creator** of the universe **refers to Himself as "The Good Shepherd,"** is not an advantageous position to be in (John 10:11). It would be wise to humbly receive His perspective and acknowledge our designated position as followers.

Unfortunately many people are unaware of the nature of the things that they follow. To follow something is to allow "it" to control you to a degree. Many allow work, family, friends, habits, hobbies, materials, and emotions to control their lives. None of those things listed know how you were created or what you were created for. So making any of those things your highest priority will put you in a detrimental position.

Because God is sovereign, He will only occupy the number one position, and because He is Holy (separate) there is no number two. Having a number two would imply that that thing is comparable with God. He is omnipresent and infinite, so everything a person may consider as a priority is encompassed by Him.

When we put God first He satisfies all of our needs and more. When a person is submitted to God, God aligns that person's being with Him and His will. In being aligned with Him we receive an order and function in our life that surpasses anything we can plan or execute.

A person may be tempted by the notion that God should just control us if He wants us to be "good." Wanting to control someone is not loving that person. How do you think you would feel if you had no control over anything you do? In my opinion there would be no point in being a conscious being in that situation. The directions and instructions in which God leads is not for His benefit; it is for us to live a good and fulfilling life.

Without proper guidance a person can convince themselves that they don't need to follow anything or anyone. That mentality is a symptom of pride. To be clear, there is nothing wrong with being a trailblazer. Trailblazers are usually led by some thing instead of some one. That "something" can be an idea, a theory, a question, a spiritual being, etc. Either way, people are followers even if our focus is to not follow.

Be careful of focusing on things "not to be controlled by." To focus on something with the intent to engage or not engage still requires attention. Which means you are giving it a place in your life. If there is something that you need to be free from, then there is something that you need to be beholden to.

Trying to "not be controlled" by something, but forming your life around avoiding the "thing," creates a conflict of interest. Without having something healthy to focus on, the person will remain unbalanced. The potential to backslide or pick up a different unhealthy habit increases.

The term "target fixation" comes to mind when I think of this. Target fixation is a physiological phenomenon that occurs when a person is so mentally and optically focused on one thing, that their body follows what they are focused on. This can occur in situations where the person is fully aware of immediate danger.

Here is an example: A person riding a bike down hill sees a tree ahead of them, then tells themselves, "don't hit the tree, don't hit the tree, don't hit the tree," but then they hit the tree. Their mind was so fixed on the tree that they didn't look for ways around the tree. Point being: We were designed to follow and what we focus on will have a physical, mental, and spiritual consequence.

Being aware of what we follow will inform us on what we are allowing into our spaces. **Spiritual spaces do not stay empty for long** (Matthew 12:43-45). The truth in the referenced scripture can reveal how a person seems like they are always jumping from one problematic situation to another. Spiritual issues require spiritual solutions and spiritual solutions can help solve practical problems. Because we are physical and spiritual beings, solutions for our issues will often have spiritual and practical components.

Recognising a problem or something that you feel is unhealthy for you is in general a good thing. Getting an understanding of how we are created as individuals will help us recognize symptoms and identify problems. It can be difficult to discern symptoms and problems when you're in the thick of it. It's even more difficult if you're following something ungodly.

Ungodly things can use our emotions against us to stir up confusion. That is not to say we should abandon our emotions. God created us with emotions so they are perfect in their creation, how we understand and handle them is where issues arise. We should be cautious in assigning emotions as problems. Doing so can cause a person to take extreme measures to "overcome" an emotion instead of addressing the problem that causes the emotion.

Let's look at fear as an example "problem." There are many people that look to "conquer" fear. Conquering something is to overtake it and control it by force. Taking by force often leaves casualties. Controlling by force provokes resistance. The problem with this case is that emotions reside internally. Committing to internal aggression will yield external aggression, and that can have severely negative consequences.

Following trends and cultures that claim to not be controlled by fear or have conquered fear, seem to actively try to instill fear into others. To instill fear you have to have fear in you to instill. So circles that claim to be fearless may be fearful. They may need help identifying where their hearts and minds are in reference to where God desires them to be mentally, emotionally, and physically.

Not letting fear control your life also does not mean to seek situations that are dangerous. The mentality of seeking fear with the goal of becoming fearless can be caused by confusion. Continually seeking mentally or physically dangerous situations can be motivated by several unhealthy things. You will find what you seek, so no matter how many "fear conquering" things a person does, if they look for fear they will find and experience fear. It becomes a vicious cycle.

Can a person become fearless? I don't know. I know a person can be courageous. I believe a courageous act is when a person recognizes their fear and continues forward with their purpose. Whether a person acts out fear or courage, the action does not permanently define them.

Fear, just like any emotion, can help us be more aware of a situation or distract us in a situation. We have a range of emotions and looking to numb or subdue any of them goes against our original design. Healthy circles are often spaces where people can process all of their emotions freely.

Sometimes our purpose may entail things that people fear, and that's fine. If God calls you to do something He will equip you with what you need. There will be times of fear and doubt, and if you fix your thoughts on Him, He will walk you through tough times. What you don't want is fear or anything else changing the course of you walking in your God given purpose.

If you are constantly doing things to prove to yourself or others that something doesn't have control, it probably has a level of control in your life. Being influenced or controlled externally can sway the way you think and behave to the point where some or all areas of your life feel unstable. Instability isn't inherently good or bad, but it should be identified. Restlessness is a reliable indicator of internal instability. If you recognize that you are in an unstable situation the ideal "next step" would be to ask God to help you navigate it.

For a person to be free from something, their mind, heart, and spirit have to be free of it. An example of this truth are people who have been incarcerated. There are many accounts of people who were released from prison, but still felt incarcerated. On the other hand there are many accounts of incarcerated people testifying that they feel free while still incarcerated. I've only heard the latter situation when people have dedicated their lives to Jesus.

It is important to understand that the things that can have a hold on us may not always have an obvious physical manifestation. They can be confined to psychological and/or spiritual habits. When we resist entertaining the "thing" mentally, it loses its influence on us. This is why **God suggests coming to Him and fixing our thoughts on Him** (Philippians 4: 6-8). Having a properly guarded spirit, mind, and heart is how we can regulate inputs. By regulating our inputs we become better stewards of our thoughts and habits.

To follow something freely you have to be free from things that you used to follow. That doesn't mean you have to abandon everything and everyone. It means you should expect changes in your habits, mindsets, and circles of influence. When you choose to follow God you do not have to "fix" yourself, He will meet you where you are. He breaks the chains of habits, and heals the wounds from our past. He will be your leader, provider, and protector. He is faithful. He is the Good Shepherd.

Follow Filled

We can only find true purpose and fulfillment by being obedient to God. He created every single thing for a purpose.

That purpose serves Him and us in the best possible way. The negative experiences of the world are the collective results of the choices we have made as a species that do not agree with His will. The instruction and love of God will break those areas of negative fear and control. His instruction will also allow us to recognize and understand truth. The truth of our situations and the truth of who we are as individuals.

God created us to live life well. We were created in His image. Do you think He wants something He created and loves to be lost and distraught? No. He is not wasteful. Every breath He gives us is an invitation for us to draw nearer to Him.

To begin to fill the void is to reestablish your relationship with God. To do that, you have to acknowledge who God is and who God sent to establish and model what is good for your soul. **God sent Jesus Christ to show and be the way to God**, to show us that all we need is God, and to pay the cost for us to reconnect with God (John 14:6-7).

This is known as "The Good News." It's called "good news" because although humans are incapable of saving themselves from sin (which separates us from God), God made a way to reconcile our relationship with Him. He accomplished this by paying for our sins. Through Him paying for our sins we have a chance to be liberated from sin and be joined with Him for all of eternity.

It is also good news because God paid a high price for it, and we can all receive it as a gift. This is known as "The Gift of Salvation." Keep in mind, the gift is free, but we still have to accept it. If you were to buy or make a gift for someone and they didn't accept it, you couldn't make them accept it. No matter the cost, value, or effort; an unaccepted gift will not be properly received. Receiving the gift of salvation is agreeing to begin a healthy relationship with God.

Throughout the Bible and this book are examples of some of the "perks" of having a healthy relationship with God as a flesh and blood human being. The scriptures also let us know that after our flesh and blood pass away there are even more. But before we pass away, there is a responsibility to honor that gift. A part of receiving the gift of salvation is to pronounce Jesus Christ as your lord and savior. Many have an understanding of what it means to be saved from something, few know how to voluntarily put themselves under a being's lordship.

To honor the most valuable gift one could ever receive, we need to do what we were created to do - follow. Voluntarily following is necessary in this case because the gift of salvation is a gift of love. Remember, love does not force its way. To choose Jesus Christ as your lord is to choose His will in exchange for yours. These decisions create tension between the inherited sinful desires of mankind and the divine desires of God. This tension is what is referred to as temptation.

Temptation is the desire to act in ways that are contrary to the will of God. As we have learned in previous chapters, thoughts can become actions, which then can become habits. God does not leave us incapable or unequipped in these situations. A part of being under Jesus' lordship is that we have access to everything we need to overcome temptation and sin in a healthy manner. Having access to something is only useful when we can locate it, and are familiar with it.

To know someone or something, intentional time must be spent. Following Jesus consistently requires reading the Bible consistently. **The Bible is the Word of God, Jesus is the Living Word of God, and Jesus is God** (John 1:1-34). This will be expanded on in a later chapter. Seeking God is to read, pray, and apply the things He shows in His word. During the journey of seeking Him your relationship with Him will grow. At the end of the day, His goal for us is to be as close to us as possible. Everything He does for us is done out of love.

One may ask "why would I want to do His will over mine?" The answer can take long to understand, but it's short in words: His will is better for you than anything you can imagine.

Better as in fame, fortune, and free from pain? No. Better in terms of knowing peace and joy in the midst of struggles. Better as in being able to lay every burden at His feet and know that He will guide us through them. Better with regard to having confident hope that there is an eternity so good that we literally need new heavenly bodies in order to witness His goodness. What does that mean? We cannot handle the full presence of His majesty with our earthly bodies, it would destroy us.

Since we're on the topic of eternity, we need to talk about the reality of sin. The reality is not pretty, but I have to share the truth with you. The cost of sin is death. Death, in the scope of eternity, is to be separated from God and everything that He is. He is love, peace, joy, truth, life, and everything that is good. To spend eternity separated from God, is to experience everlasting death in all of its forms.

Each sin has a cost of death attached to it. The cost must be paid because God is just. If a person dies with a debt of sins, they will pay the debt themselves through eternal death. Warning, our "good deeds" do not affect the balance.

Does this debt have to be paid by us? No. Jesus gave His life to pay the debt for every single person. His sacrifice satisfied the debt and gave us access to our Heavenly Father through the gift of salvation. That is how I know every breath we take is an expression of God's grace. Every moment is a chance to repent from our sins, pronounce Jesus as our Lord and Savior, and receive His gift, which is to be with Him.

Why did God put all that into one person? Because it was by one person we lost our direct connection with God - Adam. Jesus Christ is the *only* begotten Son of God and is the only person whose blood was truly innocent (completely sin free). Jesus is the only one worthy and capable of paying the cost of the world's sin. Jesus Christ is the only way for us to be redeemed from the sin nature we inherited from Adam.

When Jesus came down to Earth He was tempted to sin in every way, which enabled Him to relate to all of our struggles with sin. He overcame all temptation, which means He conquered sin. Through His resurrection He conquered death. He gave us an example on how to live a life where "the void" would **be filled** (John 4: 10-14).

God doesn't need our "grand" works or "great" gestures. He wants to be acknowledged, His Son's sacrifice honored, and His instructions followed so we can be joined with Him. A person cannot follow something that they do not acknowledge.

When you love someone and they offend you, their acknowledgement of the offense and apology reestablishes a good relationship more times than not. We are only humans, and often "I'm sorry" works for us. With the understanding that God has an unimaginable amount of love, patience, and grace for us, I hope it is clearer how He can forgive all of our sins when we apologize and ask to be reconciled with Him. **There is nothing that can separate us from the love of God** (Romans 8:35-39). In receiving Him, our "voids" will be filled.

Chapter Reflection: The Void

<u>Fertile Ground</u>

- ❖ Have you ever had an experience where you felt you had no choice? In hindsight, did you really not have a choice, or did the other option seem unbearable?
- ❖ Have you ever made a decision that you knew was wrong but you couldn't resist the temptation?
- ❖ Do you feel like there's a way to improve your reaction to "choiceless situations" or situations with temptations?

<u>The Search</u>

- ❖ Have you ever felt a void? If so, what have you done to fill that void? Did it fill the void?
- ❖ Do you feel you have to strive for everything you do?
- ❖ Are you satisfied with the work that you are doing, or do you feel like there is a purpose you haven't recognized yet?

Follow Freely

- Would you describe yourself as a follower or leader? Why?
- Do you think one role is better than the other? Why?
- What are some things you allow to control your life?
- Is there a situation or habit that you feel you were delivered from? What was/is the long term result?
- Do you think people that abet fear are fearful themselves? Why or why not?
- Have you ever experienced a situation where you wanted to do something good but then felt afraid of what other people would think? Have you overcome that fear or are you still fearful?
- Do you think God requires perfection or acknowledgment? Why?

Follow Filled

- Have you ever heard of the good news? What do you think of it?
- Reflecting on your life, do you think you are capable of securing satisfaction? Why or why not?

- ❖ Is there an "expensive" gift that you value? What about an "inexpensive" gift that you value? Why are they valuable?
- ❖ Did the gifts from the previous question come with a responsibility? Have you maintained them?

Chapter 5

Confused Communication

The human experience is very complicated. Healthy communication is a fundamental requirement for an individual, society, and species to experience the fullness of life. Unfortunately many societies and cultures do not practice or support healthy communication habits. Too often our identities and personal experiences are categorized, compartmentalized, and invalidated; for the purposes of "normalizing," industrializing, and essentially dehumanizing people. The symptoms of unhealthy communication are experienced world-wide every day, and the issue starts with spiritual health.

You can learn a lot about a person's spiritual health when you observe **how they communicate** (Matthew 12:33-37). I'm not talking about their vocabulary, diction, or ability to articulate. I'm talking about their willingness to listen with the intent to understand, and their tendency to speak kindly. Listening to understand and speaking kindly may sound elementary, but often these practices are overlooked because of their simplicity. Examining ourselves regularly keeps us aware of "simple" issues that can grow into complicated problems.

It's easy to think you communicate well and you're not "one of them;" but our ability to communicate is subjective. Standards of "healthy" communication are usually set by our environments. We are heavily influenced by our experiences, biases, and social/personal projections. Learning healthy internal communication is a significant undertaking. So when there is more than one person, things can get complicated quickly.

Considering the spiritual significance of our voice and words, one can conclude that it would be wise to learn how to listen for understanding. I believe it is very helpful to learn from people who already display healthy communication habits. Learning requires humility and honesty.

Confused Communication

Understanding and agreeing are not the same. We should try to understand the people around us even if we don't think we'll agree with them. If people cannot understand each other, the words between them can be severely detrimental to everyone involved.

Proceed with caution when reading the following paragraph. Some of you have current situations that can cause an emotional response. But the goal is to learn how to observe and be honest about ourselves regardless of others behaviors.

Think about that person you really don't or didn't like. We've all had at least one in our lives. When you don't like someone, you don't want to be in their presence or hear their voice. For the most part, they can do no good in your eyes.

I call that "white t-shirting." I call it that because it can be a warm summer day, but if a person that we don't like comes outside wearing a plain white t-shirt, we will criticize them for wearing a plain white t-shirt. The reality is that a plain white t-shirt is a perfectly acceptable thing to wear on a warm summer day, but in our mind they are in violation and deserve to be ridiculed.

This illogical response is what happens when a person holds contempt in their heart. Contempt affects the full being. With contempt the eyes and ears perceive selectively and inaccurately. In addition, basic logic goes out the window. As much as a person may feel justified in their feelings, **holding grudges negatively affects your spirit** (Ephesians 4: 31-32). If a person cannot perceive accurately or think logically, they cannot communicate well.

From my experience, many people would rather speak at someone rather than speak with someone. I believe this habit is a combination of conditioning and character. Either way, it is detrimental to true communication and I believe pride is a key factor.

Giving in to our pride will produce the habit of prioritizing our thoughts while diminishing other's inputs. Pride is dangerous because it can stop us from admitting simple truths and/or taking responsibility for things we know we should. **Pride can make us "rebels without a cause,"** and that is nothing to boast about (Proverbs 15:12). More often than not, pride will leave you looking and feeling like a fool.

That is why being humble is so important. A humble heart allows us to listen even if we feel like we're "in the right." Listening helps us understand the things around us. **Listening will reveal more things than shouting** ever can (Proverbs 29:11). You already know what you want to say, listening reveals what is in other people's hearts. Understanding people is an invaluable skill, and you cannot understand people if you do not know how to listen.

Designed Division

In the U.S.A., our society teaches us from a very young age that it's "us" vs "them." We see this in sports, politics, gender, economics, neighbors, etc. Things that could be negligible differences are often used to create false dichotomies. I say false because although people may have differences, that doesn't mean they have to be in opposition or that you have to choose one side or the other. Being continuously exposed to situations where a person feels they have to choose between one or the other creates a mindset and habit of division, even if a dichotomy is not explicitly stated.

A common topic where there are unnecessary lines drawn is male and female behavior. Men and women are a part of mankind, which means they are capable of behaving the same way fundamentally. Men can be unfaithful; women can be unfaithful. Women can get emotional; men can get emotional. Men can build things; women can build things. I can go on, but I hope you get the point.

These are things that can be observed every day, but lines are drawn in these topics every day. Unfortunately, people subscribe to those divisive narratives despite what they can see. I believe many of our divisive habits come from conditioning.

The political culture of the United States is an example of what happens when systems that promote false dichotomies are widely implemented. It seems as though healthy communication practices are not modeled or prioritized in regard to the general public. The choice many politicians make to communicate in an unhealthy manner is most apparent during public election cycle conversations. The communication of division is a systemic problem that can be observed within families' homes all the way to international seats of power.

Debates are formal arguments that can be shining examples of healthy communication in the presence of an unaligned or opposing view. Unfortunately, debates that are conducted for the highest seats of leadership in the U.S.A. teach people to argue points that they may not agree with in order to "win" an argument.

There have been many examples where politicians disregard what they truly believe in order to increase separation from their projected opponents. Too often it seems like they get "points" for shutting people down and not saying things that may be agreeable with their rival in the arena of public opinion. Think about that. Saying things with the goal of stopping others from speaking, even if they don't believe in what they're saying.

This influences people to discard their identity, beliefs, or values solely for the purpose of "winning." The "listening" that happens is only with the intent of finding points to oppose. So, a lot of what is said is disregarded, regardless of its foundation in truth or righteousness. The reality is that **if you're arguing for the sake of argument, nobody wins** (Proverbs 29:9).

One of the problems with adopting an argumentative lifestyle is that it can foster the practice of dismissing logic and morals in order to "win," even if the prize is superficial. This behavior has been normalized through consistent exposure to division. I believe self-defeating terms like "alternative facts" are birthed from a mindset and desire to "win" at all costs.

If something is believed to be a fact it can be presented as a fact, even if there is a diverging or opposing perspective. Adding alternative means the believed fact agrees with a differing believed fact for the same subject, which is impossible. You can't simultaneously agree with perceived "facts" that diverge from each other. Subscribing to argumentative mindsets builds internal and external partitions that disrupt healthy internal and external communication.

The reality is that many situations in life can be represented as a sliding scale rather than divided sections. Where you find yourself shouldn't restrict your ability to communicate in a healthy manner with someone in a different position. Having a consistent moral foundation that establishes a principle to express good will towards others helps us avoid unnecessary divisions and confrontations.

In the end, following cultural trends instead of timeless righteous principles will lead to a life of internal instability. **Without a righteous spiritual anchor, our minds will** continually change direction to **justify living in contradiction and division** (1 Corinthians 2:11-15).

So, if many situations in society can be represented by a sliding scale, why do things feel so divided? I observe a lack of honesty, empathy, compassion, patience, charity, and other attributes that the Holy Bible describes as characteristics of love. These attributes seem to be severely lacking in homes, schools, and professional settings. How can I understand you, empathize with you, help you, or give you space if I am not willing to listen to you? I cannot. If you're not listening to me, then you can't express any of those things toward me either.

This situation will inherently create a divide between us even though we may have more in common than not. It's a shame because many friendships and great things can come from presumably "odd" collaborations. How many amazing things have we missed out on as individuals and as a species because of relatively small differences? We'll never know.

The partitions of difference are a detriment to our local, national, and international communities. Although two people may be on the opposite ends of a spectrum for a particular subject, that does not mean they can't be in alignment on another subject. Allowing our differences to create divisions stops us from learning and experiencing the "whole" person(s), which is a form of miscommunication. Only reading excerpts from a book can lead to more confusion and misinformation than not reading the book at all.

When a conflicting behavior or character trait is perceived, people can have the conscious or subconscious reaction to put up a wall and disassociate themselves from a person or group. This response to difference shrinks the person's world to experiences they deem "palatable." One of the fundamental problems with that practice is that it dehumanizes humans. If a person does not see another person as a person, it is impossible for those people to communicate properly. Dehumanizing people is a destructive practice where perspective, understanding, truth, and righteousness are lost.

The truth is, every community has something to bring to the table. As much division as there is in the world, common interests like food and music bring strangers together in a way that is far greater than gathering to bicker about differences. I believe breaking bread and music have spiritual significance when it comes to people coming together.

Having the heart and mind to be hospitable can break down barriers and create a space where new friends and families form. Careful consideration should be given to how we host or enter those spaces. Those events are not incorruptible.

A healthy community should be the goal for every community (Romans 14:19). Everyone lives on sliding scales. As we learn and grow, our position on those scales can change many times. Understanding that, there is no logical reason to perpetually "stonewall" people. Understand that as a community, sometimes we will agree, disagree, and partially agree.

As a species **we are in this together** one way or the other (Romans 10:12-13). Knowing that we can rely on more than just our kin in a time of need. Knowing that a stranger can be a reliable friend. Peacefully settling disagreements, and sharing resources and ideas can improve the quality of life of everyone involved. Those are some of the fruits of a healthy community. A healthy community has to have healthy communication.

So, why are there ones willing to manipulate communities and take advantage of them? Spiritual corruption is the answer. The unwillingness to recognize, acknowledge, and communicate similarities makes for an unstable community.

An unstable community is easier to manipulate. When there is infighting, anyone or thing from the "outside" can take the treasures that no one is guarding. One treasure that can be taken from a divided community is the power of influence. A united community can change the world; divided communities are often marginalized.

Influence is a form of communication. Having influence over a population comes with temptations. Evil spirits can tempt and convince individuals or groups that having "control" over X, Y, and Z will yield something so amazing that it's worth losing their soul. They can get so caught up in these spirits where they perform, encourage, and justify horrible things like war, genocide, murder, oppression, exploitation, dehumanization, etc., for some sort of "gain."

A close-knit community (local, national, and international) would make it hard for these atrocities to easily take place or exist. So, the people that entertain these evil spirits have an interest in dividing communities. In the end, **the people that try to wield that power are never satisfied and there are countless victims left behind** (2 Peter 2:1-3). But those are examples of the extreme. In some way, shape, or form we all try to justify the wicked things we do.

That's why it's important to withhold judgment. There are plenty of awful things that take place in our urban, suburban, and rural "utopias." There are genres of "entertainment" based on "regular" people committing crime and performing horrendous acts. So we should be slow to think of ourselves as being separate or different from "them."

That's another reason why loving your neighbors is so important. Our experiences and environments influence our behavior. Many bad situations could be extinguished by being in good company. I think it's wise to engage with strangers with caution, but a prolonged guarded position without any inquiry is unhealthy in my opinion. Befriending the people around you, not just family, can broaden your social and cultural perspectives while fostering patience and empathy.

For example: If a neighbor who is usually kind were to act rude. Most people would assign the rude behavior to the neighbor having a "bad day," and not hold offense. The same situation without knowing the neighbor would most likely yield a more confrontational outcome. Consistent communication in both situations could quench hard feelings and resentment, but remaining unfamiliar with the person can turn into years of physical or mental feuding.

With all that being said, truly following God as individuals and as a community will strengthen that community and increase their resistance to ungodly manipulation - emphasis on "truly following." Religious repetition and trying your best to be a "good person" are not things that bring us closer to God. Reading His Word with child-like curiosity, praying with a repentant heart, and seeking Him personally are great ways to draw nearer to God. He is a living being who desires our hearts and availability, not our achievements.

It is very important to understand that God wants to redeem us. **God sent His son Jesus here to atone for our sins** (John 3:16-18). God loves us so much that **He is willing to wipe everyone's slate clean in exchange for simple words** (Romans 10:9-10). No grand acts or gestures we deem as "good" are needed. He will spiritually rehabilitate you for acknowledging who He is and asking for forgiveness. Receiving the Holy Spirit (through receiving the gift of salvation) is what changes people from the inside out.

Deflection

Many are aware of conversational deflection, but I just made up a term called "action deflection." Action deflection is when you have the ability to act on a situation, but deflect taking action without a logical explanation or excuse. This is something that only the person deflecting can accurately evaluate for themselves.

I know problems are everywhere and it's not feasible to ask a person to solve every problem before them. People are free to prioritize things how they see fit. However, there are times when someone else's problem is laid out in front of you and their problem is something that aligns with your skillset, ability, and availability. At that point you can deflect and miss an opportunity to help someone, or you can seize the moment. The burden of this decision can be lightened when a person seeks the guidance of the Holy Spirit.

Many of the ongoing issues of modern society are ongoing because of people that cannot see or do not want to acknowledge or address "other people's" problems. In reality, "other people's" problems will most likely become your problem. The combination of action deflection and false dichotomies can influence people to intentionally slow down or stop "other people's" problems from being solved.

This compromised mental and spiritual situation ultimately skews understanding and the prioritization of human issues. When a person does not take action in something, it naturally becomes less relatable to them over time. Combined with being on the "other side of the fence" from false dichotomy created narratives, being able to see people "on the other side" as people becomes increasingly difficult. If we can't see humans as humans it is impossible to come up with humane solutions.

When we try to push through a problem with a skewed view, the net results will be less than favorable. Some will believe that their problem should be solved first or if it's something that doesn't directly affect them, then resources should not be used to solve the problems. When that mentality spreads, forward progress is halted on a large scale.

An example of how forward progress can be slowed due to skewed views of humans is how substance abuse was/is handled in America. For many decades in the twentieth century, substance abusers in America were projected as hardened criminals, troublemakers, and second class citizens from poor, hopeless, and helpless areas. The physical and psychological segregation of the financially poor from financially stable allowed it to be politically and socially acceptable to treat financially poor substance abusers as less than human. This led to a lack of empathy towards substance abusers on a large scale, which led to a lack of resources and programs to help people in need.

In the mid-2000's substance abuse ravaged America's middle class communities. This changed the political and social perspective of substance abuse. Abusers were no longer viewed as cancers to society, but rather people with illnesses that needed help. The result was a major increase in funding and access to affordable resources to help people with substance abuse issues.

Unfortunately, the inability to see substance abusing humans as humans before the mid-2000's has and continues to negatively affect countless lives. There were/are some benefactors regarding the substance abuse industry. Unfortunately there are always people who intentionally position themselves to "benefit" from others suffering. **Gaining directly from suffering is a spiritual position you do not want to be in** (Psalms 1-2).

For clarity, I'm not anti-America. I'm choosing to speak on cultures and systems I am familiar with.

Another display of deflection is false dissociation. This is when a person does not outwardly associate and/or pretends to not care about a certain matter, but internally they are somewhat invested in the matter. To say "I don't care about ...," while having pointed opinions or emotions on the matter, indicates a space of contradiction.

If a person is not significantly invested into something, their posture should not be stern or argumentative. Why would someone falsely represent themselves? Spiritual oppression can be the root problem. **Spiritual oppression can result in communicating with anger and confusion** (1 Corinthians 14:33).

Have you ever come back from a store thinking about an item that didn't interest you? No, no you haven't. That is because the milliseconds it took for your brain to recognize that it was not something you cared for, you moved on with your life. The item could disappear off the planet and you would feel completely neutral.

Confused Communication

Now, if it was an item that caught your attention, but it didn't fulfill a need or there was a design feature that "ruined" it for you. You may have a negative response and possibly harp on the experience. That is because something in you was affected by that item. The refusal to acknowledge or inability to articulate why something influences your mood or actions can also be an indicator of spiritual oppression.

Unclean spirits encourage deflection and confusion because they interrupt healthy communication internally and externally. The less you understand about the source of your thoughts and feelings, the more influence unclean spirits can have on you. If you're stuck in anger, bitterness, or confusion for "no reason," it is most likely because you've been conditioned to deflect the need to self-reflect.

Self-reflection usually reveals why you feel the way you feel and can help you navigate your justifications. **Self-reflection is critical for understanding yourself, the state of your spirit, and finding internal peace** (Galatians 6:4-5). Reflecting with the guidance of the Holy Spirit will reveal truths that a person cannot discern on their own.

Not being willing to discover, reflect, or talk about topics can be a form of deflection. Deflection does not make problems go away; it diverts them into a "corner." Left unaddressed, those things/spirits will pile up, grow, and begin to spoil various areas of life that they aren't related to. What ties them together is the person harboring unclean spirits that exhort miscommunication and confusion.

On the Contrary

Another communicative indicator of spiritual oppression is blatant self-contradiction. More often than not, a spiritually oppressed person's words and actions contradict themselves and/or that person's interests. The contradiction occurs because their soul may want one thing, the mind can be focused on another thing, and their flesh might act out something else.

In short, their spirit is disoriented and/or confused by whatever unclean spirit they have been exposed to or entertaining. **God wants us to be at peace** (John 14:27).

153 Confused Communication

Living in contradiction is not peaceful. In knowing that God wants us to live in peace, we can deduce that one of the "missions" of unclean spirits is to disrupt peace.

When a problem is identified, it's wise to seek counsel. One cannot say, "I just want to live in peace and be left alone," and then go out of their way to aggravate, annoy, and disrupt other people's lives. When a person intentionally drives others to anger they are acting out evil works suggested by unclean spirits.

For clarity, someone becoming angry because of an action is different from performing an action with the intent to cause anger. We should try to avoid causing anger, but we cannot hold ourselves responsible for everyone's reactions. I believe we will be held accountable for actions that intentionally drive others towards anger. I don't believe the pretense of entertainment whether it be personal or for an audience will be excused either. Trolling (online or in real life), crude "pranks," and spiteful communication are spiritually unclean works that have been normalized under the mask of "entertainment."

On the topic of entertainment, saying "I don't want people to look up to me. I just want to be rich and famous," is a contradictory mindset. Wanting fame is wanting influence. To be influential is to be a role model. What you model is your choice and a certain level of responsibility "comes with the package." If you're not comfortable with the responsibility of being a role model, it may be time to pause. Take time to consider why you're not comfortable with the idea of people aspiring to follow your footsteps. Perhaps you can explore mindsets, habits, and lifestyles that you would be happy to personify.

Recognizing the need for change begins by looking at oneself. Once the need for change is recognized, it would be wise to call on God. Being spiritually oppressed requires spiritual help. Spiritual oppression yields mental and physical issues. So, seeking spiritual help can be mentally and physically beneficial.

Addicts can be **examples of people living in contradiction or under spiritual duress** (1 Corinthians 6:9-10). Addiction is a being's projected inability to live without the "thing." Addictions can start in the physical body or mind, but full rehabilitation requires an agreement between the body, soul, and spirit. It's not a coincidence that many addiction rehabilitation programs offer some level of faith-related resources and/or practices.

Living a contrary life is hard on the person and the people around them. Praying for your deliverance and praying for people that seem to be contrary is very important. It is important because the turmoil that comes with that lifestyle is serious. It's also important to not think of ourselves as "better" or without sin just because we may not engage in things that are considered contrary or immoral. We are all capable of finding ourselves in bad situations regardless of our beliefs. Anyone can be seduced by temptation, which can lead to being subjected to sin.

Many bad situations are the result of a single or seemingly insignificant, poorly-timed choice. Despite what you may think about them (spiritually oppressed people); Despite what they may think about you; The Spirit of God can redeem all. **Prayers should not be withheld** (1 Thessalonians 5:17).

Setting your mind to follow Jesus Christ with all your heart is the best way for you to defend yourself and help people overcome tempting spirits.

Blurred Vision

How can someone not see the fault in their ways when it is very clear to others? The spiritual world has authority over the physical, so disruption in the spirit is a disruption in the entire being. This disruption manifests through our minds and our bodies. When we are in spiritual duress our thoughts and bodies fail us in various ways. Our **ears don't hear**, our mouths get us into trouble, and our **eyes deceive** us (Ezekiel 12:2). Things that should be plain can become confusing, unprocessed, or unseen.

You may be skeptical of these claims, but try to think about a situation where you tried to warn a person about something that was clearly problematic, and they didn't listen. Somehow they did not see the thing that everyone "saw coming from a mile away." It could have been a lover that was "bad" for them, stealing when the only outcome was getting caught, or lying when the truth was the easiest way to handle the situation. (Admittedly, sometimes the truth seems like the hardest route.)

When we open ourselves to ungodly spirits, our perception gets blurry and then skewed. **Unclean spirits have one motive - destroy souls** (1 Peter 5:8-9). Unclean spirits live in a higher "dimension" just like good spirits. Their understanding and perception of things are above ours, and they are more intelligent than we are. They will entice us with things that seem good, but they use those things as bait for our trust. Their goal is for us to let our guard down and give them authority in our lives.

Once they have authority, they will pick a person's spirit apart if left unchecked. They are methodical, well-equipped, and extremely experienced in manipulating mankind. They are a more cunning adversary than any human can handle on their own. When they are given a place in a person's life, that person will most likely find themselves in a significantly compromised position before the severity of their position is fully realized. This is not a fear tactic; this is just the reality of the situation.

When a person's spirit is bound and/or blinded, so will their flesh and blood be. The terms "blind rage," "blinded by greed," "blinded by love," and "fueled by envy," are symptom descriptions. They describe **what happens when you give an ungodly spirit authority in your life** (2 Corinthians 4:3-4).

"Blinded by love" is the idea that a person does things against their better judgment because they are in love. When it comes to love, it is imperative to seek clarity from God. True love is not harmful and it does not take advantage. True love does not create confusion, cause blindness, or deceive. True love comes with truth and clarity.

The truly negative experiences associated with being in love are not rooted in love. The negativity comes from a variety of things. Spiritually, unclean spirits recognise the potential for true love to occur. Their response to a situation where true love can occur is to disrupt and destroy.

That is not to say we don't have a part in our negative experiences. We should take responsibility for our choices. Unhealthy practices and habits learned from popular culture are a very strong adversary as well, because they can influence our choice.

Many people are blinded by lust, fear, hopelessness, and/or idolatry disguised as love. When you worship a person whether it be a lover, parent, child, friend, neighbor, mentor, coworker, celebrity, historic figure; any person that was or is on this earth except Jesus Christ, you are submitting yourself (which includes your vision) to unclean spirits.

Loving and worshiping are not the same. Loving someone may be summarized as giving with a kind heart without expecting to receive. Whether it be time or resources, it is when a person shares themselves with another. To worship something is to live for the person or thing. Worship is a position of servitude. What we worship and how we worship will influence our perception.

Unhealthy worship can look like an enabling parent, a workaholic, or a lukewarm Christian. All of these situations can begin with a healthy level of dedication, but decline in health over time. With time passing the person may not be able to see how far they have deviated from their original path. It's important to know that anything in the hands of a human can be corrupted, even dedication.

A dedicated parent can turn into an enabling parent. Which means that child can do no wrong in the parent's eyes. This is a very spiritually dangerous position for the parent and child. **Living without limits or reprimands creates a rotten individual** (Proverbs 13:24).

A dedicated worker can turn into a workaholic. When a person buries themselves in work, they may be dealing with some internal struggles. In burying themselves in work they may not be able to see the other components of their life falling apart.

A dedicated Christian can become lukewarm if they lose sight of Jesus. When a Christian leans towards their personal desires and preferences opposed to looking to be led by Jesus in all things, their focus can begin to blur. As time passes the more and more lukewarm they will become.

In the context of Christianity, lukewarmness doesn't just occur from half-hearted commitment. It can also be produced by jumping between extreme levels of dedication. A room that fluctuates between forty-nine and fifty-one degrees will have the same average temperature as a room that jumps between zero and one-hundred degrees.

I think most people have a grasp of what half-hearted commitment looks like, so I'll briefly speak to the other kind of lukewarmness. A person living a double life is an example of jumping between two extremes. In some environments the person has the appearance of living biblically righteous while in others the person is unkind, self-serving, and continually engages in behavior that contradicts Jesus' commands.

Now none of us are perfect, and there is grace for being genuinely unsure and making honest mistakes. What we don't want to do is become blind to our ways. **We should examine ourselves** often because over time indecision becomes a decision, and living a double life is a contradiction

(2 Corinthians 13:5). Lukewarmness is overcome by living a consistently congruent life.

It is very difficult if not impossible to adjust our focus without some sort of external gauge. Being in a healthy community can help us calibrate our perception if things get a little blurry as we walk through life. In addition to being in good company, we have to be humble enough to receive the message that our perspective may be skewed. The best optometrist in the world can't help a patient that's not willing to get their eyes checked.

That is why choosing who is in your inner circle and your significant other should be taken very seriously. Whatever spirits they entertain will have a large amount of influence on you, your other friends, and your family. The old saying "show me your friends and I'll tell you who you are" acknowledges the influences we can have on each other.

As I said earlier, the reality of the spiritual world is plain to see. We reference and experience it every day. Seeing and beginning to understand it is a matter of inquiry.

It's a matter of taking the time to pause and ask questions, self-reflect, and disregard fruitless inputs. Learning how to stop accepting every input that is in front of you is an important life skill. Filtering and taking the time to digest the things you receive on a daily basis helps with overall clarity.

Our worldly culture is rush, rush, rush, go, go, go, because **evil spirits run wild in this world** (Ephesians 6:12). They know that if they can rush us, they can have their way with us. A clouded, messy mind will not find clarity or peace.

When our mind cannot find clarity or peace, we can be distracted from looking towards God. In that scenario, we default to relying on our flesh and blood, which is the worst thing we can do as spiritual beings. That's why the Bible tells us to continually **renew our minds** (Romans 12:2). Renewing means clearing out, cleaning up, and replenishing.

When you're not filtering and clearing out the things coming at you, it's like driving in the rain without your wipers on. The faster you go the less you see, and the more dangerous it becomes for everyone near you. Crashing is inevitable. Don't get caught in the traps that evil things set before you. Clarity, freedom, and peace are the results of following the spirit of God.

The Ear of the Beholder

Listening is a muscle of the soul that should be exercised by everyone. The more you listen, the more you hear. Listening is not restricted by physical hearing. There is no medium God won't use to communicate. Be patient, you will hear. If you look and listen for God, He will reveal himself. Keep your peace.

True discernment starts at the ear - not your physical ear, your spiritual ear. Discernment comes with biblical understanding, prayer, and practice. Listening for what things are living for is the core of discernment. In other words, discernment helps reveal motives and heart postures. We can only listen for these things accurately when we receive wisdom, understanding, and guidance from The Spirit of Truth.

Confused Communication

Often we use our eyes and ears to build context composed of what we see and hear. Understanding context is vital to discernment. Context is only understood by practicing patience, accumulating perceptions, and leaving your projections to entertain themselves.

Regularly exposing ourselves to The Truth by engaging with God and reading His Word (the Bible), we can learn how to discern the truth from what we don't physically see or hear, too. The flesh and blood practice of this is called deduction. Deduction without spiritual understanding and guidance is incomplete.

Though the ability to discern is a gift, the ability to discern without the will to accept truth is a waste. Discernment comes with a test of the heart. It is a test because when the truth is revealed to that person, it is their burden to reveal or not reveal the truth. Will the person reveal the truth despite the outcome for themselves? How will they time the revelation or concealment? What are the motives behind their actions? **The ability to discern is a blessing that incurs significant responsibility** (1 Kings 3:9).

In all communications be careful of what you speak, watch, and listen to. Understand that when you express a want or need, spiritual beings will respond. The content of your expression can direct who or what will have authority to enter your space. That is why we should use extreme caution with our words and what we give authority to.

Wisdom will teach you that praying for God's guidance and prescribed provisions is far greater than praying for things and outcomes. Waiting in God's word is more important than I can express, and listening is a requirement for being obedient. This is why our ears are fixed open, but we have a choice to open or close our mouths.

Chapter Reflection: Confused Communication

Introduction

- Do you think you're a good communicator? Why?
- Do you think you're a better listener or speaker?
- Have you ever "white t-shirted" someone? Why? Do you currently feel justified in your action(s)?

Designed Division

- Can you think of a situation that you would consider a false dichotomy? Expand on how it's a false dichotomy and how it can plant the seed of divisiveness within an individual or society.
- Can you think of a situation in society where there is division?
- Have you subscribed to that division by picking one side and stonewalling the other? Why?
- Do you find yourself arguing for argument's sake? Do you think this is healthy?

- Have you ever been in partial agreement with someone from the "other side" but refused to acknowledge it because they were on the "other side"?
- Do you think a "good friend" always agrees with you?
- Do you have someone who holds you accountable for your actions, good and bad?
- Have you ever been in a heated argument that ended in a civil compromise or understanding?

Deflection

- Have you ever exercised "action deflection"? How do you feel about your actions or inactions now?
- Can you name a problem where the resources are available, but the problem is not being solved?
- Can you name a problem in society that you feel resources are being wasted on. Why do you feel it's a waste?
- For the problem you listed above, does it involve you in any way? (Keep in mind the problem, not the solution(s).)
- How often do you self-reflect? Do you think self-reflection is important for personal growth?

- Do you think people should only solve their own problems? If so, how do you think that would work in a modern society?

On the Contrary

- Are there any areas of your life where you feel internally conflicted? What is the conflict?
- Have you ever called on God to help you resolve your problems? How patient were you?
- Have you ever intentionally bothered people for your personal entertainment? Do you think that's okay?
- Do you have a circle of influence? How do you think you influence that circle?
- Have you ever made a poorly timed decision that had a greater impact than you anticipated?
- Do you see how one poorly timed decision can put anyone in a "helpless" situation? Why or why not?

Blurred Vision

- Have you ever been in a situation where a negative outcome was obvious, but you couldn't see it until after it was done? If so, why do you think you stayed in that situation as long as you did? Do you recall if anyone tried to warn you?

- ❖ Have you ever seen someone, or have you put someone on a pedestal where it had a negative effect on you and/or the people around you? What was that experience like?
- ❖ If you absorbed all the habits of the people in your circle, would you be in a better position or worse position?
- ❖ How often do you feel rushed or unable to find moments of peace or clarity? Why do you think that is?
- ❖ Do you schedule "down time" or do you try to keep busy? Why?

<u>The Ear of the Beholder</u>

- ❖ When encountering a problem, is your first instinct to find a solution to the problem or to understand the problem?

Chapter 6
<u>The Problem with Evolution is... Humans</u>

There are several secular theories of evolution. A shared belief in these theories is that all life on Earth spawned from a single cell organism living in the ocean. Over an extensive amount of time (billions of years) it evolved via mutations into everything that has ever lived. Traditionally these theories completely reject "creationism," also known as "intelligent design."

Evolutionists' rejection of creationism leads them to have a firm stance in believing that everything on earth happened by chance. I find several insufficiencies with these theories in general. When they are used to "prove" creationism and/or the God of Abraham are not the cause for our existence, a double standard for logic and curiosity is often present. At the same time, I don't believe that science should be taboo in the Church.

In the Beginning

To start this conversation, let's talk about the beginning of things. I believe this is the best place to start because just like many things in life, as time goes on, things can get complicated. To state the obvious, I was not there at the beginning (big surprise right?).

This means that I have some questions that may never be answered, and I'm ok with that. I think it is good to ask questions even if the answer is never found because at the very least I can recognize and acknowledge what I don't know. I don't believe we should shy away from asking hard questions whether they be questions of faith, science, or other. I hope I remain curious through this life, and I definitely have some questions that I believe only God can answer.

When it comes to secular evolution, one of the areas where I have questions about is the daily life of an "incomplete" creature. That is, a creature that has not evolved in any way relating to the theory of evolution.

The Problem with Evolution

Food is something that every living being requires, and many things eat many things. So, here are some of my questions: How does inorganic material become organic? Can proteins exist without organic matter to start with? What did these "simple" beings eat? Where did these food sources come from if life was just beginning? Did these beings live off of one or multiple food sources? Is photosynthesis something that "just happened" in the beginning or is it an evolved ability? How did they scavenge or gather these resources? How did they test what was edible and what was poison without dying? Were they able to observe and communicate their findings with other evolving single cell beings? How does an evolving single cell organism change its digestive system to accommodate the new being it's trying to become; while still maintaining its current means of energy consumption? Why would a microscopic being form a more complex digestive system that relies on other beings? How does the unevolved being change its innards to maintain life within itself (digestive bacteria) without getting consumed or poisoned by the newly introduced life within itself? If the single cell beings were able to eat, multiply, and live as they were, what motivated them to evolve?

I also have questions regarding the introduction and sustainability of the first single cell organisms. How did these first creatures change from inanimate particles to living creatures? If they came as "seeds of life" through space, wouldn't at some point earlier in time they need to change from inanimate to living? Was it single or multiple beings that came to be? If there were more than one, were they the same "type" or was it a variety that spawned? How or where did the concept of survival get ingrained into living beings? Where does the desire to propagate come from if there is little to no benefit in regard to survival for the being that is already living? Do reproduction processes vary between single cell organisms? What is the longest life cycle of a single cell organism? What mediums do these cells thrive or survive in? Have those mediums changed since the beginning of life? Have we recorded a being that has transformed from single cell into multiple cells within itself? How does a seemingly "mindless" instinct-driven creature become cognitive? Do these "simple" creatures rest?

These questions I have are genuine. At times where I think about the vastness of time, space, and life, there is a point where my brain, body, and heart says "enough, I'm starting to melt," and I rest.

In a time of meditation and reflection, I stumbled into something that I believe to be true. Random does not exist. I believe the word "random" is a word humans created to describe patterns that we don't recognize or understand. I believe it is a word that we use as a placebo to comfort our pride because admitting that we don't know or don't have the capability of ever knowing can be very unsettling. I believe "random" to be a theory that we have mistakenly accepted as truth. It seems to me that every observable thing in our universe indicates some sort of pattern, which would mean random cannot exist.

With that being said, that doesn't mean we cannot explore and discuss theories or theories that rely on other theories. I believe asking questions in good faith and listening for understanding is important for healthy communication and vital for healthy communities. For the rest of this chapter I will share my thoughts on the topic of secular evolution.

Are We There Yet?

I think a logical approach to this topic is to start with some of the things that are offered as "evidence" that God did not create life on Earth.

The fact that many species share some similar biological markers is a popular talking point to try to invalidate creationism. It is claimed that inward and outward biological similarities found between aquatic and terrestrial life indicate a "natural" evolution that couldn't have been created. The issue with that theory is that sharing a similar design and/or component(s) is not an indicator that something was not designed. In fact, similar designs are more likely an indicator that the said "things" were designed (I'll expand on that later).

The idea of life starting in the ocean does not go against Hebrew and Christian beliefs. Both spiritual texts

(Torah & Holy Bible) state that the first living things on Earth were **an abundant amount of life that started and came from the ocean** (Genesis 1:20-21).

Note: Hebrew and Christian beliefs are bound together. "The Old Testament" in the Christian Bible is the combined books of the Hebrew Bible, the "Tanakh" (Torah, Nevi'im, Ketuvim). "The New Testament" in the Christian Bible, documents the fulfillment of the promises given in the Tanakh.

The evolutionary theories agree with the spiritual texts in terms of the order in which aquatic and terrestrial life began inhabiting Earth. So, it is not clear to me why life starting in the ocean is presented by evolutionists as an opposing point to Christian creationism.

Theories in evolution also suggest that random mutations and an extensive amount of time are the cause of our existence. To suggest that all life comes from single cell organisms randomly mutating is unsound. Random by definition is unstable, and random does not regard time. Therefore things that are truly random are constantly unstable on every level regardless of the scale of time. If our existence were truly random, that would mean every atom in the universe would be unstable indefinitely. Instability cannot produce stability and random cannot birth intent.

Mutation in the context of evolution is categorized as a random occurrence. Mutations are medically known to be more problematic and harmful than helpful. It should be understood that mutation and adaptation are not the same.

Mutations are changes that happen in a creature's DNA sequence that is usually credited to an error on a cellular level. Adaptation is the ability to biologically adjust to environments. Exposure and conditioning to environments can produce some levels of adaptation, but there would have to be a "safe place" for the being to return to in order to accommodate the time it would take to adapt. Swimmers increasing their lung capacity is an example of this "in and out" conditioning.

In order for mutations to be helpful or adaptations to occur, intent is necessary. As capable as humans are, we don't have the ability to naturally change one hair on our head. For the world as we know it to form solely by mutation and adaptation, beings would have had to mutate their own DNA to grow wings, expose themselves to arctic temperatures to survive arctic temperatures, and their transformation would have to be a result of their own will.

For evolution to occur on Earth's scale, two factors would have to be available: an extensive amount of time and an extremely stable environment for that entire length of time. Time happens naturally and perpetually (from a human perspective) so there is no restriction there. Stability is where the theories are lacking viability.

Earth's ability to sustain life is relatively delicate. The temperature and the chemical balance of the atmosphere and ocean are four factors of many that are vital to sustaining life on Earth. A small deviation in one can greatly affect the other, which can cause severe environmental oscillations.

Geological studies suggest these factors have not been stable for billions of years collectively or independently. To suggest that an organism could not only survive for billions of years, but also thrive, develop, and mutate into "improved" single and multiple cell organisms during global scale volcanic eruptions, earthquakes, flooding, ice ages, shifts in atmospheric and oceanic composition, and environment disrupting meteorites can be considered negligent at the least. One of the stated natural disasters could be considered an extinction-level event in modern times. Less evolved creatures surviving multiple extinction level events would be highly improbable, especially considering the fact that some of these events happen over a relatively short period of time.

New & Improved

The mainstream theories of secular evolution share the belief that the evolved being is better adapted to the environment than its predecessor. If that were true, mankind would become better adapted to their environment as time went on. Let's explore that idea.

The theories presented suggest that mankind evolved from "lesser" primates such as apes. Several primates have the ability to greatly outperform mankind in just about every natural environment, today. To try to negate that fact, it is suggested that mankind is a more evolved being because we seem more capable mentally. Yes, our capabilities have allowed us to create technology, which sets us apart from the rest of the animal kingdom. The issue with our "superior evolved ability" is that it is literally killing everything in the environment, including us.

Evolution stands on the premise that the more evolved is better suited to survive the immediate environments. We (humans) are not doing that at all. Building walls, a roof, heat, and air conditioning is not surviving the environment; it's changing the environment to a very specific environment for survival. On the surface, this could look like "the ultimate evolution ability," until you realize that it destroys the natural environment. This leads to lacking resources, which leads to extinction. Changing or destroying an environment is not thriving in the environment. One could argue that those actions are the fundamental indicators that something is not natural.

If humans were to find or terraform a new life-sustaining planet or system, we would still cause an imbalance. Changing from a balanced creature (the rest of nature) to an imbalanced creature (humans) is not an improvement. Nor does it agree with what can be observed in nature.

In studying nature whether it be a rainforest or molecular structures, it can be observed that just about everything (living or "inanimate") has the natural tendency to move towards being balanced. Considering the **destructive things humans consciously do to each other**, how can a "superior evolved being" be the reason for its own demise (Proverbs 10:2)? How can "inferior" beings (literally everything else on Earth) have the ability to sustain themselves perpetually, but not the "superior"? Secular theories of evolution are found flawed through the existence of humans

Design & Development

Earlier in this chapter I touched on how similarities across many species in terms of bone structures, organs, and other physiological markers, denote design opposed to random mutations/events. When it comes to design, whether it be functional or aesthetic, similarities can be an indicator that the component or assembly was crafted by a particular creator or manufacturer. Sometimes similarities are designed into the creation specifically to show that they are a part of a series of work. On the consumer level, design signatures are known as "branding" and/or "design cues." We can see these in almost any line of products we use daily.

Let's look at vehicles as an example. Externally, with the labels and badges removed, many people can determine a manufacturer or series of vehicles based on design cues. This is because most manufacturers intentionally choose distinguishing exteriors so consumers will know exactly what they are looking at in terms of brand and capabilities.

Internally, it may be more difficult to distinguish the manufacturer. This is because the components in every vehicle interior have to meet a certain level of function, and if you're in the car, chances are you know what you've gotten into. So seats, the steering wheel, and other control mechanisms may start looking similar to other manufacturers. There are some that stand out, but this is a general conversation.

Looking deeper into the vehicle with the lens of function and operation. Vehicles use similar if not the same electrical, electronic, and mechanical components and materials as refrigerators, flashlights, sofas, and T.V.s. All those devices look, operate, and function differently, but they share components between all of them. These are things that have a creator or creators. As a matter of fact, they all can come from the same manufacturer, plant, or even the same designer.

The same logic manufacturers use to create man-made goods can be applied to the natural world. God can create whatever He wants, however He wants. If He makes an organ that works for animal X, why is it unbelievable that He would use a similar design for animal Y? In my opinion it's not unbelievable because mankind does that every day.

On the other end of the spectrum, the differences between species is an interesting topic of this conversation that is brushed over often. How can animals that are so different evolve from the same origin in the same environment? If survival is the goal of evolution, then things from the same region should be relatively similar and/or have a goal of becoming an apex creature.

This is considering the theory of everything evolving from a single cell "non rational" being. One of the problems with the theory is that sustainability and balance are cognitive, intentional decisions. You can find a lion, beetle, crane, and giraffe sharing the same environment for millennia and they remain very different and maintain order.

One could say, "They are different because they have different functions to sustain the environment," and I completely agree with that statement. The conflict with evolutionary theories is that wild animals maintaining order does not fit the "survival of the fittest" principles. That phrase is one of the pillars of evolutionary theories.

Following the survival of the fittest principal, things would evolve for their survival, not everything's survival. Evolving into a groundskeeper or prey is not ideal for a being that is committed to a "survival of the fittest" environment. Across the globe very different species work together in extremely organized systems. How can a jungle filled with millions of different creatures sustain a balance far greater than anything that "evolved" men have created? A supreme creator is the only logical answer.

Plot Twist

Many creators and scientists outwardly reject God as the creator and the idea of intelligent design, but if you look at what their ambitions are, they try to be just like Him. To say that there is no way something created "this" and "that," while at the same time trying to create "this" and "that," comes across as being obtuse in terms of self-awareness. Many of the limitations that men try to put on God are projections of insecurity and fear. **Humble yourselves** (1 Peter 5:6).

In terms of mankind's ability to create, mankind's greatest achievement would arguably be creating artificial intelligence. A being that can perceive, interpret, react, and change without commands or presets. A being that makes choices based on its own experiences and self-awareness. Mankind's projected greatest achievement would be the thing they say God can't create. We are the "artificial intelligence," and we decided to take a wrong turn.

This is why **applying** science **without God guiding your mind yields destructive results** regardless of "good" intentions (Ephesians 4:17-19). Many of the things mankind has created can be used in so many great ways, but at some point the technology ends up stunting our ability to improve as a species. We are rich in capability but poor in compassion. Laws about data collection pass faster than laws about feeding children. When you leave God out, you leave good out. **With God we can use our minds, abilities, and gifts to**

help each other, and the world would be a better place (Romans 12:3-5).

To ignore the many examples of how God is the creator and harp on "what if-isms" or focus on things that are still a mystery to mankind as "proof," is not ethical or scientific. One could ask, "If God knows, then why won't he just tell us?" He tells us many things through the Bible, but if you reject what He has already said how can you expect to receive more? This **lack in seeking inhibits** many from **comprehending** what is in front of them (John 3:10-12).

With modern technology we are able to study things that were viewed as "simple," and now know there are many levels to the most "basic" things. The deeper we dig, the more we realize we don't know. As a matter of fact, many single-cell organisms and their operational systems are still unknown to us.

All that to say, I think we all have something to contribute to our society for the better. There are many beautiful, brilliant people that have been blinded by pride, hurtful experiences, deception, or ungodly motivations. It's healthy to ask questions if you are willing to receive the answers. It's natural to respond to mystery and the unknown defensively, but we should not shut out opportunities to grow in areas that have boarded up for the sake of comfort. This is encouragement for the scientific and religious communities - never stop seeking truth. We should be cautious to block things out based on the premises of "normal" or traditions.

For me, science provides proof of our creation. Observing the world grows my relationship with God because His brilliance, artistry, precision, and expressions of love are everywhere. There is not a painted sky or a grain of sand that lacks His creative signature.

Chapter Reflection: The Problem with Evolution is...

Humans

- In reflecting on this chapter, is there anything you took away? Is there anything this chapter inspired you to investigate?

Chapter 7
Carbon Copies

I'm going to draw some parallels. Mankind currently has a great sense of pride because of our collective achievements. When it comes to creators, we talk about our creations like they're our child. We literally use the phrase, "It's my baby," when we refer to a project or creation that we pour ourselves into. We refer to our work as if it is a part of us. We spend our time, energy, and other resources refining these projects to make sure that they are the best versions of themselves. In addition, if a function or feature becomes obsolete we will most likely try to update the creation.

These mannerisms of personalization and association are not products of coincidence. These are not phrases, mindsets, or habits that "came out of nowhere." They are an essence of our Creator that He has sewn into us. We were designed to receive and exhibit His nature.

God refers to us as His children because we are His creations that He loves. He controls time and energy for our wellbeing. Any "updates" we need to get aligned or re-aligned with Him, He has already set in place. **He will keep those who are His up to date** (Amos 3:7).

When it comes to our creations, the better we get at creating, the better the creations are at adapting. The first automobiles were considered novelty machines. One term used was "horseless carriage," which was generous considering at that time horse-led carriages were very refined and relatively comfortable. On the other hand, cars at that time were not. They were slow, high maintenance, unreliable, noisy, nasty, and terrible in inclement weather.

Fast forward to the present, cars have improved greatly in every way. In short, they can be extremely comfortable and literally change with the environment. Modern cars know when it's dark, they know when it's hot or cold, they read road conditions, and they respond to driving styles. Some have the ability to make adaptations virtually instantaneously (faster than we can perceive). Bad weather?

Active driving aids improve vehicle stability. Sleepy? "Driver, wake up" or "let me (the car) drive" systems activate. Need better cornering or braking? Active aerodynamic components move and shift to improve performance. We are at the point where vehicles change their outwardly and inwardly appearances and functions to adapt to their environment. Point being: Our creative abilities and creations are lesser forms of His creative abilities and creations.

We reflect and in some ways try to be like God. Some efforts are conscious decisions while others may be behaviors and principles that we are less aware of. Our communication goals certainly reflect a desire to be God-like. For example: individuals have the technology to see and talk to a person that is on the other side of the world. A person or organization with greater resources can view, listen, and interact with many people in different locations at the same time. This is a lesser version of God's omnipresence.

Adaptive vehicles and advanced communication devices are a few examples of how we are God's "carbon copies" (metaphorically and literally). Personal association with creations, ability to design, adaptive mindsets, and pseudo omnipresence are indicators that mankind is infused with God's creative posture. We should receive the understanding that as we are less than Him, so are our creations.

Sowing Seeds

In this modern era, we have the ability to manipulate and synthesize sources of food and energy. When it comes to food, we have found ways to improve crop yields, increase resistance to disease, and manipulate flavors. Despite our personal preferences, healthy synthesized supplements can be very helpful for getting people properly fed.

In terms of energy manipulation there are many natural and synthesized options available. Different methods can be optimized for different environments. Considering these two areas of development, the ability to provide healthy food and energy for everyone on the planet is very possible, today. Unfortunately, that is not the direction we are going.

It can take an entire field of study to explain how mankind has corrupted farming, access to healthy food, and energy distribution. In short, poison is readily available for consumption, natural foods are becoming a delicacy, "living off the land" is becoming less plausible and/or illegal, and the world has been at war over energy for decades.

Despite great technical developments, abilities, and resources, many people starve and/or freeze to death because of the "human factor." My definition of the "human factor" is this: "The tendency to corrupt a system by replacing the initial intended purpose and/or motivation of said system, with a deviated purpose and/or motivation that is contrary and/or unrelated to the original." This is an observable occurrence in almost every system that humans interact with. I encourage you to consider the systems in your life, society, and workplace with the "human factor" in mind. With that being said, the "human factor" is a result of being born in sin, which implies spiritual corruption.

From my observation, there seems to be a mindset that leads people to assimilate an "all or nothing" mentality.

This mentality can be seen in a variety of discussions, especially discussions concerning what many consider "basic" human rights. This form of polarization can come from unclean spirits that promote selfishness, division, and greed. Those are all components of the human factor.

Let's look deeper into the topic of energy. We can start from a personal perspective then expand from there. When you need energy, you either eat, drink, or rest. What you decide to do and how you do it depends on your environment and personal situation. It would not be good to sleep while running or eat while you're swimming; there can be negative consequences to those actions. When it comes to energy production and distribution for a "modern society," the same general principle can apply. The general principle is that decisions should be made based on the surrounding environment, sustainability, and people. Considering all people as human beings is where I feel we fall short as a species.

When it comes to energy resources, some would get along fine with a solar powered house, a diesel powered car, and a work facility powered by fission. For other regions, those methods may not work in their environment or be sustainable for their situation. So, choosing alternative systems such as wind, water, coal, and natural gas could be logical options. All of these energy systems are ok in moderation, just like eating and sleeping.

To have an all or nothing mentality in this subject is not logical because there are many possibilities and opportunities to find compromises. Polarization in this topic has led people and organizations to act in relatively extreme ways. There is no moral logical reason to try to hinder or impose preferences when there are a variety of plausible options available. I understand that infrastructures need to be in place for certain things to work, but that doesn't mean it has to be one or the other. This is truer as the scale becomes larger. There are many energy harnessing and distribution systems possible. Unfortunately only a handful are implemented and made available to the public.

I believe one of the stumbling blocks of society in this conversation is the focus on controlling markets and manipulating public opinion. Shifting the focus from discovery and understanding to "securing a profit" changes conversations and execution in many ways. When the focus is on harnessing and distributing energy, the majority of the resources go into just that. That means focusing on improving efficiency, lowering environmental impact, and improving distribution methods. When the focus shifts to controlling markets, many of the resources go into bribing politicians, buying out patents to stifle innovation and competition, covering or containing legal issues, and feeding an insatiable hunger for power and control. A business does not have to have a perpetual increase in profit margins in order to sustain itself.

The world would greatly benefit from having access to energy related resources without the strings of greed attached. There is no easy solution to the problem we have dug ourselves into, but every solution starts with correctly identifying the problem. The global energy problem isn't really about energy, it's about money and power. The corruption of systems and manipulation of public opinion is at the point where people who would be negatively impacted by a one-sided system will advocate for that one-sided system. The human factor is dangerous because its root is Godless. We cannot free ourselves from ourselves, by ourselves. As individuals and as a species we need divine intervention to operate healthily.

To be clear, I think many systems mankind is involved with can and have had positive outcomes. However, I think we either neglect or are overconfident in our understanding. Often we create with a heart full of pride and sometimes ignore or are ignorant to the possibility of negative repercussions. Too often personal gain is prioritized over the greater good, and in the end it all turns bad.

We can be better than that. We don't have to constantly be in opposition either. These poor decisions are the result of not having God as a navigator. If we lived by the principles God has given us and practiced the lifestyle that Jesus was the example of, we would be less self-centered and the things that have the potential to be good would have a better chance of staying good. The principles and examples can be found by reading and studying the Holy Bible.

In the end, all the things we create are lesser versions of what God has already created. Our achievements are lesser versions of things He can already do, and that's ok. That reality aligns with us being inferior creatures emulating our creator. To be the best version of ourselves, we should acknowledge and receive His imprint on us. We are carbon copies.

Chapter Reflection: Carbon Copies

Intro

- ❖ Have you ever obtained or created something that you referred to as "your baby" (besides a child)? If so, why did you feel such an attachment to it?
- ❖ Can you think of an object or product that mankind has designed to be adaptable?
- ❖ Do you understand why there is an Old Testament and a New Testament in the Bible?

Sowing Seeds

- ❖ Can you think of a system where the definition of the "human factor" applies? If so, what do you think the original purpose was, and what do you think it's driven by now?
- ❖ Have you ever started something with a purpose in mind, but by the time it was done, the outcome and/or purpose of the thing was different? How do you feel about that?

- Was that outcome or change related or unrelated to the originally intended purpose?
- Do you think the changed purpose was beneficial or detrimental to the intended audience?

Chapter 8

Just a Man

Fighting Against Flesh

You'll see recurring themes in the Bible, life, and as a result of those, this book. The reason why is because God is faithful. He is consistent even when we are not. Because He loves you and wants to have a relationship with you, He will say the same thing in different ways. If you feel like you have been running in circles in some aspects of your life or all of them, it's most likely because you can't discern His voice or you're not listening to what He has told you. Believer or non-believer, trying to do it "your way" will yield results that lack true peace and fulfillment. **He's waiting for you with the best instructions possible in-hand** (Revelation 3:20).

Our flesh fights against the spirit of God because it is born in sin, which means it has a sinful nature. **The flesh will try to convince you to do the thing that is ungodly because that's all it knows** (Romans 8:5-8). That resistance to God and godly things is called temptation. We have to choose to turn our minds and hearts towards God and receive authority over our flesh in order to break ungodly cycles. Even when a person is fully submitted to God, their flesh will resist godly things until they pass. Does that mean we are powerless against temptation? Absolutely not. Remember, the spirit and the mind have a higher authority than the flesh. The thing is, authority is only useful if you receive it and know how to use it properly.

Not receiving and applying the authority that God has for us may lead to situations where we feel like we don't have options. At times **we may feel like** circumstances push us into a corner where **there is only one way, but** this is not true; **we always have a choice** (Proverbs 14:12).

We may not see all of our choices in a flesh and blood mindset, but they are there. Sometimes the other option(s) may seem so undesirable or unbelievable that we convince ourselves that they are not even an option. Pride and fear are usually strong factors in those situations. I encourage you to not let pride, fear, or any unclean spirit inhibit you from applying your authority in making decisions.

The truth is we all make poor choices. It's easier to make poor choices when following flesh and blood desires. Poor choices can lead to bad habits, which can then turn into a troublesome lifestyle. Often the original desire fades away, but we can find ourselves continuing the act(s) because doing things habitually can cause a person to become numb to the results of their situation (good or bad).

It's important to understand that the things that make you feel bad morally the first time are most likely things you should not continue to do. Repeating the action is not going to change the reality of the action, but it can condition you to abandon your morals which makes you feel less conviction. You can try to convince yourself that you are happy or that the actions were justified, but from time to time you will feel the truth of not standing on good ground. Those periodic "nudges" is God asking you to turn from those ways.

I believe we are born with a sense of morality. I believe this is why we feel bad about things that we weren't necessarily told were bad. I also believe that our sense of morality can become significantly callused at a relatively young age.

The cycles of poor choices, broken lifestyles, self-abuse, and self-loathing can be broken with God's help. Admission to these issues are vital for breaking those cycles. From personal experience and observation, it seems many struggle with recognizing and/or admitting they have an issue. In recognizing and receiving Jesus Christ as Lord and savior, **His moral compass is written in our hearts and our sins are forgiven. This is a part of the New Testament** (new promise) (Hebrews 10:11-16).

People usually reduce pride to being conceited, but there is another fruit that stems from the branch of pride - stubbornness. Stubbornness is just as detrimental as conceit. Conceit is being deceived to think you are superior to others. Stubbornness is a deceptive mindset that rejects and dismisses the thoughts of others. Both of these characteristics grow calluses around the mind and heart which distorts the communications that are received and sent.

The distortion caused by pride amplifies the agreeable inputs while muting the disagreeable inputs. Only receiving agreeable communications leaves no room for calibration. Over time the person will have a mind and heart that echoes "I am the way, everything should agree with me." This amplified message is then output through words and actions.

That is why communicating with a prideful person can be draining. It takes more energy whether it be via higher frequency, higher amplitude, or both to get a clear message across their internal echo chambers. I believe that a prideful person struggles with expressing what they view as an internal fault or failure for the same reason. I think it parallels trying to remember a song while a different song is already playing - you may remember the idea behind the song, but the rhythm and the lyrics escape you. You try really hard at first and then out of frustration you realize you either have to turn off the song you're listening to or decide remembering the other song isn't worth the effort.

Reflecting on God's grace has guided me to pray for more patience when dealing with prideful people. I can and have been prideful many times, often unbeknownst to me. The fruit (symptoms) of pride is attached to the fallen nature of our flesh and blood.

As we reflect on our own journey we should humble ourselves and acknowledge that we can be deceived by our own desires. This gets tricky because sometimes we attach our unclean desires and motives to something that appears as righteous.

Here is an example: most people don't want to be viewed or view themselves as stubborn, so they may mask their stubbornness as diligence. Stubbornness and diligence are not the same. Stubbornness pushes through situations with no regard to our senses and outside information. Diligence seeks information from various resources, even if it seems like it is in opposition; then navigates the situation with understanding and resolve. Rejecting stubbornness is a requirement for breaking self-destructive cycles.

Some other symptoms of pride are deflection and unjust justifications. An example phrase of an unjust justification that is commonly echoed is, "if I don't do it, someone else will." **This is a lie that unclean spirits suggest to persuade a person to do something that they don't agree with morally** (Psalms 37:7).

The false justification may be tempting for various reasons, but the net result will not be good. Accepting that mindset will increase the influence unclean spirits have in your life. Whatever that thing is, leave it alone. **Trying to justify your sins because of someone else's sins is not justifiable** (Psalms 37:1-2).

As discussed in previous chapters, our words have consequences. Many people accept their stubbornness and other fallen behaviors as a part of their identity, but God created us to reflect His character. When we are deceived by unclean spirits we take on unhealthy habits and identities. **We need God's wisdom to help discern the habits and identities that inhibit our positive spiritual growth** (2 Timothy 2:24-26).

There are many stumbling blocks and lies that people believe are a part of life or their core character. Time and repetition without examination of self can result in a person abandoning their core character. If there is a habit or "personality trait" that you don't like about yourself, then you are most likely dealing with a deep seeded lie that was suggested by unclean spirits in one way or the other.

Stop claiming "this is who I am" when it's something you don't like or agree with. God gave every single person a good character when He created them. Since we are born in sin and evil spirits are relentless, these stumbling blocks could have been instilled early in childhood by a number of things. **Ask our Father in Heaven to break unhealthy cycles inhibiting your life** (Romans 13:12-14).

When we choose to do something that goes against what we know is right for the sake of our pride, personal gain, or "for sport," it takes us away from becoming the person that God created us to be. God wants us to be the best versions of ourselves, which is a person that exudes **the fruit of His spirit** (Galatians 5:22-23). **Giving into seducing spirits is an act that will yield results that go against your interests** (Proverbs 11:4).

Fire and Brimstone

There is a misconception that God is waiting for people to mess up so He can "rain down fire and brimstone." That is simply not true. If you read the Bible, you will see that God has more patience and grace than any being. **Even when people perform horrible atrocities, God gives everyone, every chance possible to be forgiven of their offenses** (Ezekiel 33:11). He's even held back angels from avenging injustice in order to give people a chance for redemption. It's up to us as individuals to make a choice between repenting or rebelling.

"Free will" is a phrase that many people seem to step in and out of when it is convenient for them. Some people will marvel at themselves when they make choices that seem to have a "good" outcome, but, when things go south they ask, "How can god allow this to happen?" Free will applies to good and bad decisions, and the outcomes of our decisions are not always instantaneously obvious.

God places the good path before everyone. Sometimes He'll even give you that "gut feeling" that you knew you should have listened to. Free will is the power of choice. We have to accept that sometimes it is more than we can handle, and that's ok. We also have the choice to ask God to help us with our choices. His grace has no end.

Implying that God is looking for reasons to hurt people or cause issues in our lives is a misunderstanding. These ideas and projections can be the result of experiencing some sort of trauma. Hard things happen, and sometimes we cope by lashing out. Lashing out can be a natural first response, but **it is not good to rest your mind on anger** (Ephesians 4:26-27).

If left unchecked, a person can become consumed by their anger and continue to lash out beyond the root cause. Sometimes the anger remains focused, but many times the anger infiltrates other areas of life. This is because when a person harbors negativity, unclean spirits will try to take advantage of them in their weakened emotional and mental state. But know this, God is not eager to cause harm to His creations, and He will meet them wherever they are.

In All Fairness

The term "fair" gets thrown around a lot without having a true grasp of what it means. It's not uncommon to hear someone say, "If god was real or good how can he let bad things happen to innocent or good people? It's not fair!" People often ask this question when referring to tragedies concerning children or loved ones. I understand the pain of loss. God-led grieving is the only way to truly heal those wounds.

For the sake of this conversation, imagine God deciding to "step in" and stop anything "bad" happening to children (under 20 years old). This would mean they would be completely immune to "bad" things like injuries, ailments, poverty, foul language, hurt feelings, nasty food, odors, and the list could go on. Essentially children would be indestructible and their emotional experience would be pure joy or nothing for the first twenty years of their life.

What would happen when they turn twenty and have their immunity removed instantly? It would in no doubt be an extremely dangerous and traumatic situation. Because they are immune to "bad" things, there would be no way to prepare them beforehand. Informing them of the realities of losing their immunity would be a negative experience. So not only would they not experience the "bad" things, they would be ignorant of them too.

I can only estimate that the mortality rate and the complete collapse of mental health in young adults would become astronomically high. They simply wouldn't know how to operate in a world with negativity or consequences. The population that did survive the transition would most likely feel that taking away their immunity was "unfair" and most likely become envious of children.

In the end, the same complaints about fairness would be present. The combination of free will and actual fairness is what we experience more often than not. The "good" or "bad" choices we make can have a good or bad impact. It is not clear to us because our perception is so limited. Children and others may be innocent, but they are affected by their environment just like everyone else, which is fair by definition.

Yes, **God has the power to do whatever He wants, whenever He wants** (Revelation 22:13). You have to consider that His perspective is something that humans cannot fathom. **Our understanding** of good, bad, neutral, early, late, too much, too little and a million other things **is meaningless compared to God's understanding** (2 Corinthians 12:9).

The choices that we make as individuals have a real effect on the world and it's impossible for us to foresee the full repercussions of our choices. We collectively experience results from choices people have made and are making. Subsequently, we influence the current and future experiences of others.

So, if a tough situation occurs and you feel tempted to speak poorly of God, stop right there. Consider the fact that we can't truthfully prescribe a situation or being as "fair" or "unfair." Reflect on the fact that we cannot comprehend the full context of events that have happened, are happening, and are going to happen. Ask God in the name of Jesus about your situations with the heart to truly seek understanding. More often than not, you will get clarity and peace for the situation.

One of the things Jesus accomplished while He was flesh and blood on Earth was to experience life as a human and live perfectly. He experienced every temptation, extreme poverty, loss, rejection, and injustice. **He knows what we've been through and has overcome it all** (Hebrews 4:14-16). My suggestion is: Before you criticize His character, seek His true character diligently. The more you engage with Him, the more you will see His truly good nature.

Good, Bad, & Other

There is something very important to understand about how we perceive "good" and "bad." We are not equipped to fully comprehend good and bad independent of God's wisdom. Therefore, we don't have the ability to judge good and bad from our own intellect. From a human perspective, good and bad are subject to opinion and time.

What may seem "good" in one moment can turn "bad" in the next depending on your perspective. Ultimately we may never know the net result of our actions as individuals or as a species. That is why we should look to God for direction in all matters. He is truth. He defines what is good and what is bad.

He stands outside of time. He is the only being capable of casting righteous judgment. All good things come through Him. Which means if a being were to make a righteous judgment, it would be through His direction; whether they are aware of His influence or not.

When we try to take a position that is greater than we can bear, things get misaligned. This is why theories in ethics are divided. Combining ethical theories tends to create paradoxes. The combined results are often inconclusive because when you have stern restrictions mingled with limited perspective and comprehension, the likelihood of coming to an agreement is very low.

It seems like mainstream psychological academia categorizes spirituality as a mental construct for coping and/or survival. The common belief is that spirituality is just a means some people use to manage life psychologically, but ultimately the spiritual realm is not considered to be a "real" thing. I believe this approach can distort understanding the foundation of the human mind and leave out context which can be fundamental in developing ethical philosophies.

To better understand our species and experiences, we need something to "fill the gap" of perspective and knowledge. Minimizing or excluding the spiritual context of millenia old belief systems, biblical proclamations, moral codes, and documented events; is detrimental to our ability as a species to navigate the complexities of "good" and "bad." Partial context can be dangerous because an uninformed perspective can distort the truth to the point of inversion.

To that point, many people view death as the ultimate bad, the final punishment; the end of everything. This widespread perspective is a result of the full context of death being unknown. Mainstream societies seem to have the tendency to summarize things that are not understood as bad. But, we should not be fast to label situations. What needs to be understood is that **things that are "bad" according to this world, aren't necessarily bad when you let God lead your life** (Romans 14:8).

This may be hard to receive. Consider the idea that death is not always bad or a punishment. **Death can be mercy and/or a reward** (Luke 23:39-43).

It's very possible that God spares people from terrible experiences by calling them home (death). Death can also prevent someone from becoming a terrible experience. To be absent in the body is to be present in the spirit. **When a person passes**, at some point **they** become conscious in their spirit and **find themselves in the presence of God** (2 Corinthians 5:10).

When a child passes, they are not responsible for their actions on Earth because **God is graceful and does not hold immature minds accountable** (Romans 5:13, John 9:39-41). This also applies to individuals whom God determines as being innocent in their understanding, regardless of age. His judgment is just. They spend their eternity surrounded by the love of God. This is a love greater than we can imagine.

Sometimes we are able to observe our lack of understanding good and bad in "hindsight" situations. This is where a person reflects on an experience or scenario and is able to note moments, information, and/or decisions that could yield useful information to the person reflecting.

For example: not getting that "dream job" can seem like a bad thing at the moment. After time passes, you may find yourself in a great situation that would not have been possible if you did get the "dream job." In that situation, hindsight revealed that the "bad" thing was actually a good thing. It is also important to know that not every good or bad result will be observable.

It's not unpopular for people to curse God because they believe He orchestrates the "bad." If a person believes God is real enough to curse Him for the "bad," then the person should consider that He also orchestrates the "good."

Since many consider living an overall good situation, in that mindset it wouldn't be illogical to praise Him for every breath that we take.

Note: If living doesn't seem like an overall good situation, I encourage you to seek God and counseling, sincerely.

Life is a gift. God informs us of unclean spiritual entities that hate humans. These entities can manipulate emotions and distort perspectives to convince people that God is the "bad guy." What really happens is that God calls us to walk on a righteous path that He created for us as individuals, and unclean spirits suggest unrighteous decisions. What we choose to do as individuals determines how we experience God's will being done on Earth.

God doesn't make a person do anything they don't want to do, and He is sovereign. So His will will be done, but if you are not in alignment with Him, your experience won't be the experience He wanted for you. Our assessment of our experiences are heavily influenced by our perspective.

Not being aligned with God distorts our perspective. A distorted perspective can cause a person to fight something that is the best thing for them. These distorted actions and reactions of individuals will influence their surrounding environment.

The decisions we make as individuals have collective results. To blame God for our collective actions is an irresponsible and illogical mindset. Sickness, death, and many truly negative things are results from our ungodly behavior as a species. Because our comprehension of good and bad is very limited we should try to withhold the judgment of others, including God.

The truth is we all fall short of being truly good. We are all guilty of being bad at some point. If you can't acknowledge this truth, you are most likely in a room of pride, and the virtue of being humble has been knocking at your door for some time.

In the end, it should be understood that **the sentence we will serve is not based on the summation of our**

actions; it is based on our willingness to repent from our sins and follow God (Ezekiel 33:12-16). If you are willing to submit yourself to Him, He will give you everything you need to be in alignment with Him. Pray for guidance. Ask Jesus to open your mind and your heart to Him. Exercise humility by breaking the habit of operating by our own understanding. Follow the principles and examples of righteous living written in the Bible. Leave the judgment of good and bad up to Him.

We should focus on the other components of life like learning how God created us (identity), godly obedience, how to share our gifts and talents with others, and thinking of ways to positively influence our communities and environments.

Chapter Reflection: *Just a Man*

Fighting Against Flesh

- ❖ Have you ever felt like you were running in circles in an aspect of your life? If so, has that cycle been broken? How?
- ❖ Have you ever been in a situation where you felt like you only had one choice? If so, what's the context?
- ❖ In hindsight to the question above, were there other options?
- ❖ Have you ever done something that you felt bad doing the first time, but after repetition, you stopped feeling bad about it? If so, why do you think you stopped feeling bad about it?
- ❖ Have you ever used someone else's sin to try to justify your sin? Did it make you feel internally conflicted?
- ❖ Is there a habit or character trait that you don't like about yourself, but you accept it as a part of your identity? If so,

what have you done to improve or change that habit or character trait?

Fire and Brimstone

- ❖ What is your definition of free will?
- ❖ Do you think free will means there are no rules or consequences? Why or why not?

In All Fairness

- ❖ Considering the ripple effects of our choices, do you think we (humans) have the full capability of defining "good" or "bad"? Why?
- ❖ What is your definition of fairness?
- ❖ In a world where we have free will, do you think your definition of fairness is possible? Why?
- ❖ Do you think it's fair that people suffer from other people's decisions? Why or why not?
- ❖ Do you think it's fair that people benefit from other people's decisions? Why or why not?

Good, Bad, & Other

- Do you believe there are fates worse than death? Why or why not?
- Have you ever experienced a "hindsight" situation where things seemed bad but turned out good?
- Have you ever experienced a "hindsight" situation where things seemed good but turned out bad?
- Do you think God requires good deeds to receive His grace? Why?
- Do you think grace requires action for it to be given?
- Do you think forgiveness requires perfection?
- Think about a person you consider to be a "bad" person. Do you think they view you as a "good" person? Why or why not?
- Would you submit yourself to their judgment? Why or why not?
- Should they submit themselves to your judgment?
- Do you think there is a difference between observation and judgment? Please elaborate.

Chapter 9
<u>More Than a Man</u>

When a person acknowledges that the God of Abraham is **God, acknowledges that Jesus Christ is the son of God, accepts Jesus Christ lived, died, and rose from the dead to be their Savior, and asks for their sins to be forgiven by Jesus**; God gives them the gift of salvation (Romans 10:9-13). This gift connects us to the one who is more than a man, Jesus Christ.

When you receive Jesus Christ as your Lord and Savior, you commit your entire being to God. This means God has the rights to you no matter what was done before acceptance, and **your soul and spirit will be renewed** or "born again" (John 3:3-5, 2 Corinthians 5:17). Having a soul and spirit that has been renewed by Christ makes you a new creature with a new nature. This new nature frees you from the sinful nature we are born with, and allows God to move in you and work through you in ways that were not possible before. It's important to note that being born again does not make you better than anyone, but it does mean you are different from those that aren't.

The soul must be made clean and the spiritual body made new because the soul and spiritual body were born spiritually unclean. Clean and unclean cannot exist in the same space, and to be called God's children we must be made clean. Jesus Christ offering himself as a sacrifice was the only way we could have the opportunity to be made clean. Being made clean spiritually does not mean the flesh is clean and/or incapable of sin; it means our sins are forgiven. Once the sins are forgiven, the relationship between man and God can begin to be fully re-established.

Once our spirits are renewed by the Holy Spirit, water baptism is how believers identify with Jesus dying and rising from the dead. Being submerged in the water symbolizes death, and re-emerging from the water symbolizes resurrection. Water baptism is a sacred spiritual act, and should only be performed when a person recognizes Jesus Christ as their Lord and Savior. With the soul, spiritual body, and conscious renewed by God, **that being is given**

authority over sin by the power of the Holy Spirit (Romans 8:9-14).

It is important to understand that **Jesus was sent so we could be redeemed** (John 13:8). When He sacrificed Himself and overcame sin and death, a new covenant was established. With the new covenant established, He was sat at the right hand of God because His work for that season was completed. As He sits by the Father He sends us provisions for us to utilize until His second coming. **One of the many Heaven sent provisions is the Holy Spirit** (Acts 2:38).

The Holy Spirit is the Spirit of God. The Holy Spirit can provide help to any situation at any time. He can help with healing, peace, insight, understanding, provisions, knowledge, guidance, strength, hope, clarity, and anything else that is righteous in God's eyes and aligns with God's will. **You can only successfully call on the Holy Spirit after receiving the gift of salvation** (John 14:12-17). **If you do not receive God you cannot use His spiritual authority**

(Acts 19:13-16). The Holy Spirit is a being with great spiritual authority.

The Father, the Son, and the Holy Spirit are the only beings that have righteous authority to be prayed to (Matthew 6:5-13, Philippians 4:6-7, Ephesians 6:18, John 14:13-14). A believer's prayer should be directed to them and them alone - no angels, no apostles, no mothers, no ancestors, no statues, no images, no trinkets, no man, no created thing, nothing else. Praying in the name of Jesus and asking the Holy Spirit for help with your prayers is how I suggest to communicate with GOD.

Jesus Christ is a name and a title that only one being is worthy to bear. Therefore, when we say Jesus (with the son of God on our mind) or Christ, only one can honestly answer. In the presence of an authority, calling a title is like calling a name; Christ (the anointed one), Jesus (deliver, rescue, salvation). He has been given several names and translations of those names, but do not argue over which is "better" or more "accurate." The Lord knows the hearts of men and as a result He knows when you are calling on Him, even if you cannot speak. **Abstain from being contentious** (Titus 3:9).

Three and One

I'd like to start this section by sharing a truth with you; no created being can fully understand the non-created being that is God. Humans, angels, puppies, and kittens are not exempt from this truth. The awesomeness of our creator extends past the depths of the universe. Considering that truth, there is an eternity of things we can learn and engage with waiting for us.

Bringing it back to a more comprehensive scale, we haven't experienced living fully in the spirit. So there are many things that will be revealed after death. Until then we can look to the Bible and ask the Holy Spirit to guide us so we can try to get an understanding of the things unseen.

The Holy Trinity is a term that many have heard of before, but may have not meditated on it. The Holy Trinity is

God presented as three persons. There is **God the Father, God the Son, and God the Holy Spirit** (Matthew 28:19).

How the Bible reads is that **the three are one** (John 10:30, Ephesians 4:4-6,1 John 5:7). **God the Father is** the deity God that is holy, sovereign, and **the creator of the universe** (Job 38:4-7). God the Son is Jesus Christ, also the deity God. **Jesus is the word of God that became a man** (John 1:1). **The Holy Spirit is** the deity **God that is a spirit** (Genesis 1:2). This can be difficult to "wrap our heads around."

Common questions are: "How can one become three while remaining one?" "If they are one, why did Jesus refer to the Father and the Holy Spirit as if they were separate entities throughout scripture?" "Why did Jesus say that He does what the Father tells Him if they are one in the same?" "Why did Jesus say He had to go away in order to send the Holy Spirit if they are one?" I think these are all great questions. Let's try to unpack this in a digestible manner.

From scriptures we read, **man was made in the image of God** (Genesis 1:27). What image means from God's perspective and to what extent of an image we are is not known to me, but it gives us biblical context to contemplate. So let's look at the physical human body and its basic form and functions to try to get an understanding.

God the Father is the supreme being. He defines all things and all things are under His authority. From a biological perspective, God the Father sounds like a brain. The brain does all the processing and tells everything else what to do. Everything is connected to and under the authority of the brain. In one way or the other the brain knows everything that is going on. As a side note: our brains have subconscious functions, but God the Father is all-knowing so nothing is hidden from Him.

God the Son is also referred to as the Word of God. What does it mean to be a word? Words are the foundation of communication. There are multiple ways to communicate, but they all try to convey a word or message. Biologically this sounds like the nervous system; where signals flow through the body. Woven with the brain and every part of the body, the nervous system is the key for thoughts to become actions. Without the nervous system, there is a disconnect between the brain and the other body parts. The brain works with the nervous system to send instructions and receive responses from the rest of the body.

God the Holy Spirit has many names, several refer to a type of work or position of work. The advocate and **the helper** are a few names associated with the Holy Spirit (John 14:26). Also, when human figures in the Bible performed miraculous works, it is said that the work was done by the power of the Holy Spirit. Biologically speaking that sounds like the rest of the body. In general, the parts that perform work inside and outside of the body. These parts also connect inputs from outside of the body to the nervous system, which lets the brain know what is going on externally. What we know from the academic study of physics is that when a body performs work, that work can be expressed in units of power (if time is given).

I hope this analogy clarifies how three distinct entities can function as one. They can share the same identity and nature. Having the same identity does not mean they cannot have different positions, functions, and names.

For example: If I was in a group photo but the only part of me in the photo was my arm, I wouldn't refer to my arm as just an arm. I would say "oh that's me right there" or "that's my arm, I must have been cropped out." In this case, a piece of me represents all of me and the rest of me is unseen. The people that were present would know that the arm was mine, but a person who wasn't there would have to investigate in order to find out whose arm it was. Through investigation the person could learn my name, where I could be found, and how to get to know me.

Note: These are examples that may make it easier to comprehend how three can be one. I, nor anyone else can fully "describe" God, His being is beyond our comprehension.

Continuing the analogy of "God as a body," let's expand our understanding by "zooming out." Imagine a piece of paper with two horizontal lines on it. These lines divide the paper into three sections. Each section represents a space. The section at the top is the "God" Space. It's a space where God stands alone, it is simply beyond us. The middle space is the spiritual space, and at the bottom is the space we are most familiar with, the tangible universe.

God, being the creator of all things, means He has the authority to do anything He wants in those spaces. I'd like to walk through biblical scriptures to visualize what they would look like when they are applied to this "God as a body" model.

In The Book of Genesis we read that God **the Father,** God **the Word, and** God **the Holy Spirit were present in the beginning** of creation (Genesis 1:1-3). When the Father spoke, things were formed. Using the body model, what that would look like is the brain giving a command, the nervous system communicating with the rest of the body, and the body performing the duties. On the piece of paper with the three sections, it looks like the body reaching from the top section through the other sections and creating things in their respective positions. All these things can be done by the Father while He remains in His "God space."

How can He be in all three spaces at once? Let's look at the roles again. **The Father makes the decisions and gives instruction** (John 14:26). **The Word communicates** (John 14:24). **The Holy Spirit brings power**, which is an expression of work (Acts 1:8).

For things to be created there needs to be a plan. Those plans need to be communicated and worked out. All communications and actions in the spiritual and tangible spaces can be carried out by the Word and the Holy Spirit. God the Father never has to "leave" His space. With the three-section paper in mind, imagine His Word flowing through the sections like a vapor, and materializing things according to His desire. He is absolute.

Next, let's try to visualize what the conception and life of Jesus would look like from this perspective. The scriptures say that **Mary conceived by the power of the Holy Spirit** (Matthew 1:18). Which would mean God the Father spoke, the Holy Spirit received the communication, and then constructed a vessel (a human body) to house the Word. This "house" was created inside of Mary's womb.

How can you house a word? The famous "Hollywood" sign is a physically constructed word. It was created to convey a message. God being *the* Creator, He constructed His Word beautifully. So when Jesus Christ was on Earth in the flesh, He was God's Word living among us, conveying messages.

In the New Testament, **bodies are** referred to as **temples** (1 Corinthians 6:19). Temples are houses for worship. We are also houses, and we were created to worship God. We can worship God by sharing His messages.

In the scriptures, Jesus says that **He says what the Father tells Him to say** and **He does what His Father does** (John 12:49, John 5:19-23). He delivers the messages of His Father's kingdom and shares the fact that He is the Kingdom. He is the Father like how my arm was me in the cropped picture. When Jesus was here in the flesh He showed mankind a "glimpse" of the unseen God. That "glimpse" was enough to change the course of eternity for every person who has ever lived.

Jesus performed miracles through the power of the Holy Spirit to fulfill and complete the fundamental message of the old testament prophecies: repent and seek salvation. So what I see in the conception and life of Jesus, is our Heavenly Father telling His earthly children, " I see you, I am with you, and I love you. Follow my Word and be made whole."

Finally, let's look through this lens to visualize the promise that the Holy Spirit is being sent to live-in and work-through mankind. It has been established in the Bible that one of the reasons Jesus was sent was to set an example for humans to follow. To follow would imply that we should operate how Jesus operated. So using the paper with the three sections example, it would be God sending a human the Word, the person would receive the Word because the Holy Spirit lived in them, and by the power of the Holy Spirit the human would do whatever was spoken.

Now here is what needs to be understood, the Father, the Son, and the Holy Spirit are one and are always in agreement with each other. So everything within them and their works are flawless. We were not born perfect or with that relationship. Most are born without the Holy Spirit. Depending on the environment a person is born into, they may not be exposed to the Word either. What that would look like is a person existing in the middle and bottom sections of the three section paper, with no godly life in them; with God the Father constantly sending messages in various ways to get the person to receive His Word.

When a person is exposed to His Word and receives His Word, the Word sends the Holy Spirit to create new life in that person. This is what it means to be born again! Referring to the "God as a body" model; when we are born again it's like we are grafted into His Body.

The Holy Spirit makes the person a new creature internally (soul and spirit) and when you follow His instruction (mind and body), that new life can be experienced externally. So when we receive the Word, a.k.a. Jesus Christ, we receive a relationship with God to where He can communicate and work in us and through us.

This is amazing because now instead of having one person (Jesus) sharing God's messages and works, many can. Regarding the paper with the three sections, we see God the Father on top and a tremendous amount of beings connected to Him in the spiritual and tangible sections. This is why the Church is called "The Body of Christ." In being a part of the body of Christ everyone has a position in His body. Jesus is the head of this body, so all members should be getting direction from Him.

To be clear, "The Church" is not buildings or structures. The Church is composed of people who have received Jesus Christ as their Lord and Savior. In receiving the gift of salvation, the individual becomes a temple where the Holy Spirit lives. Attending church (as in the events that typically happen on Saturdays and/or Sundays), is the gathering of the Church and people seeking to find their identity in God.

In receiving the gift of salvation, a person gives up their spiritually dead, individual identity, and commits their being to be joined with the body of God. In doing so, they receive a new identity through Him. Being a child of God is the foundational identity of every believer.

The flesh and blood things we associate with our identity in this life like our occupation, marital status, and parental position will eventually fade away. Being a child of God is an eternal identifier. It's very important to seek an understanding for yourself of what being a child of God means. In doing so you will start to become equipped to live like a child of God. Standing on that identity will give you the solid ground to fill the roles and responsibilities God calls you to.

Now if all this talk about spaces and bodies, and where the body's belong, and whose body is who's, leaves you feeling a little confused; take a breath. The Bible makes it plain for us. **Jesus resides in God the Father, so if we reside in Jesus, we also reside in God the Father** (John 17:20-21).

New Navigation

The Bible tells us that when we agree to become children of God, He adopts us into His family. In being adopted into His family, one of the ways we can think of God is as a parental guardian. God being our spiritual legal guardian means He is invited and involved with everything that we do as His children.

Understanding that this is a family that we have been adopted into, it would be wise to share our daily experiences. Look to receive good counsel, and learn to trust Him for our care and protection in all situations. God being our legal guardian also **gives Him the consent to present and operate on our behalf** (Romans 8:26-28).

This position also includes a level of protection against unclean spirits. Prior to becoming His, many spiritual beings had some level of access to our being (physically, mentally, and spiritually). It is important to know that being His does not mean we are physically, mentally, or spiritually "bullet proof."

Remember, God is fair; not just in this world, but also in the spiritual world. Receiving the gift of salvation saves our soul from being damned after physical death, but we are still subject to the consequences of our choices. The principles that establish the relationship between physical and spiritual are still relevant; **continue to respect them** (1 John 1:5-10).

When a person is born again, the dynamics of physical and spiritual experiences change. **Having accepted the spirit of God, the person receives spiritual authority to cast out unclean spirits** (Mark 16:16-17). This is why a person does not need to "get themselves right" before giving themselves to God.

God has the power to overcome everything. So the things that may have had a hold on us can be overcome by Him, and thus, setting us free from the bondage of sin. Because of His love, grace, and mercy, people can receive Him wherever they are in life, and begin their journey of transformation for His glory. He does not leave us the same.

The manifestation of changes can be mental, spiritual, and physical. Changes in attitude, desires, and feeling conviction or guilt during and after committing a sin can occur relatively quickly. Habits and addictions may end abruptly or take time and effort to overcome, but they will be overcome. The dynamics of your relationships may change as well.

It is important to understand that He will equip a person with everything they need to sustain righteous living. It's our responsibility to choose Him as our number one priority continually. Jesus has to be Lord over our lives in order for us to overcome tempting spirits and sin consistently. The processes and times for these transformations are determined by the person's submission to Him and His grace. His grace is sufficient.

Navigating our personal experiences and habits while interacting with the rest of the world is a life-long journey of learning. It should be understood that breaking the habit of just listening to ourselves and relying on our own understanding is not something that happens overnight. As flawed human beings it takes us time to receive, process, and enact certain things. Thank God for His patience and grace, and let us pray to live with patience and grace towards others.

When it comes to navigating life, here is something that I've experienced to be true - when we are obedient to God, He multiplies the impact of the steps we take. **An obedient step towards God is better than any amount of work we can do on our own** (1 Samuel 15:22). Obedience to God is an act of love and worship. God blesses obedience.

True North

God created each one of us with a specific plan and purpose. The path He creates is the best possible way for us to go. Because God created the plan and purpose, they are inherently holy.

This infers that His plan includes us being submitted to Him, because you cannot walk a holy path without being made holy. We are made holy by the blood of Christ. Which brings us to a simple point, He wants to walk with us.

This has been true since we were created. It is critical to understand that God wants your heart above all things. Our very being was designed to be in a close relationship with God as a Father and us as children.

To be in a healthy relationship a person should have a good handle on their identity. This will allow them to understand their position, expectations, and avenues of communication. The truth is that in the process of becoming an adult in this world, many people lose sight of who they are at their core for various reasons. Many put on characters as they move through different seasons, and sometimes they either forget, don't realize, or refuse to take them off.

These characters we put on hinder us from walking the path we were meant to walk. To walk a path created by Truth, we have to know who we truly are by being freed from the lies that lead us to put on characters that we were never meant to be. Learning who we are and who we were created to be can only be drawn out by our creator, our Heavenly Father.

Being submitted to God like a child to their father allows Him to teach and prepare us for the path He created for us. Like children, we have to learn how to think, behave, communicate, and walk in a way that represents our family. Once we've given ourselves to Him, He begins this process of aligning our being with His.

What's amazing about the process is that the more we learn about Him, the more we learn about ourselves. We were crafted to live with Him. So the full extent of our being can only be brought to life when He lives in us. The more we live for Him, the more alive we become. The fruits of this new life are the products of Him unveiling our true identity to us. This is what is referred to as finding our "identity in Christ."

Another amazing thing about having God as a father is that He supplies everything you will ever need to accomplish what He asks. So throughout the processes of reform and renewal He gives us the energy, patience, understanding, strength, and rest to become our best selves. In order to receive what He offers we have to "show up" in the way He tells us to present ourselves. He is able, we have to be willing. I must reiterate that in every "move" we should seek to have His love as its foundation. **Without love, actions have no value,** and God is love (1 Corinthians 13:1-3).

At this point we have been exposed to the truth that we need Him in order to understand our true identity and align our being with His. He is our "True North." Let's take a step back and look at some fundamental things we can ask God for and put into practice. These are things that will help establish a firm foundation in our hearts and minds so we will continually seek a close relationship with Him.

The first thing to do is accept the gift of salvation. This is where the healthy relationship begins. This is an exciting milestone. Your soul is secured to experience eternity in Heaven with God. The Body of Christ celebrates this and all of the heavenly beings celebrate when your soul is saved. Praise God. Rest in this security and know that nothing can take this gift that was given to you.

The next thing I strongly suggest is to get a Bible and become a student of it. Becoming a new being and being born again means there's unlearning, relearning, and new learning around how to live. The Bible equips us. We get to know God's character and how He speaks through reading His Word. Reading the Word daily also gives you sustenance to transform our hearts and minds. No daily bread = no energy/food to keep our growth going.

Before reading, ask God to show you what He has prepared for you every time you read, even if you've read the text before. Pray for wisdom and understanding of His word. Pray to receive everything according to His will. Read the scriptures SLOWLY with the intent to understand. Highlight and write down the things that "pop out" to you. Write down your questions and thoughts. Pray and seek for safe resources and people that may help answer your questions and process your thoughts.

The Bible is the only essential resource and/or doctrine for knowing who God is and how to have a healthy relationship with Him. Every resource outside of the Bible may help our journey, but they are not essential. This book is not essential.

So how do we vet outside (non-Bible) resources? By being a student of the Word of God and relying on the Holy Spirit's guidance to navigate our steps. Doing this will give you a firm foundation to safely explore resources, people, and communities.

If you get exposed to spiritual things that are not of God, you can turn to God to seek the truth of what you have seen and/or heard. One biblically sound indicator of truth is that the resource, person, or place points to Jesus Christ as the *only* way to connect with God, and agrees that the Bible is the only essential resource.

In regards to people, we should be willing to engage with all kinds of people and communities, if we are called to them. Living in isolation is not only clinically unhealthy, it's biblically unsound. Finding and engaging with a variety of communities is what believers are called to do, and there are many benefits to doing so. It's not good for people to be alone.

God fosters exchanges with others. God created us as individuals, but even as individuals we are a part of a collective body. In regard to godly communities, one of the benefits is that you can share and receive wisdom and understanding. The things that one person is called to do can help and work with things that others are called to do. Another wonderful benefit is that you can gain friends and family.

That being said, followers of Christ are called to engage with communities outside of the Body of Christ. The call to secular communities will be based on the individual and led by the Holy Spirit. Our calling will most likely lead us to secular communities where our presence makes an impact. We may not always be aware of our impact so it's important to remain sensitive to the Holy Spirit's guidance and faithful to our assignment.

Old mindsets, habits, and unclean spirits may try to distract, distort, or disrupt your understanding of what the Spirit is leading you to do; abide in Christ. Even in our call to engage with secular communities, we should still be connected with our godly communities. Our godly communities help keep us grounded and equipped to serve our secular assignments well.

All those things you just read are related to being a student of the Bible. Good students work out what they have learned, regularly. Now I'd like to share what I have learned that can help us stay diligent and aligned with God during our study. To be clear, this is a lifelong study.

My journey has led me to believe that there are two components of faith that we should seek to live out with every breath. We should seek to love God with our entire being, and we should seek to live with the fear of the LORD. A part of **loving God is to obey Him** (John 14:15). A part of **fearing the Lord is to hate evil** (Proverbs 8:13). To get a fuller understanding and apply these values, pray for them.

Fearing the LORD is not like fearing anything else. It is a fear that strengthens our resolve when encountering temptation. It slows us from being quick to respond with anger. It fosters humility and patience. It reminds us to lead in love and not hold offences. It urges us to seek His will and not pursue our own. It is a blessing that grows our trust and dependence on Him. The fear of the Lord draws us closer to Him.

From the beginning to the end, the Bible is filled with scriptures that reckon loving God and the fear of the LORD as being essential for anyone who wants to have a close relationship with God. These two components are like the left and right rails of a train track, and they are tied together by the living Word of God, Jesus Christ. These "rails" keep us on the path that leads to the Kingdom of Heaven. Centering ourselves on Jesus helps keep us stable throughout our journey. We should regularly pray to understand, receive, and live in agreement with these values.

Calibrated Compass

I cannot tell you the details of your journey. I believe this visual can give some structure to your thoughts, and hopefully an understanding of how we should try to function. Please reference the "tethers" diagrams while reading through this section.

Imagine a metal bar. At both ends of the bar are loops where a chain can be connected to them. In the center of the bar there is a hole where if a pin were put through it, it would spin freely.

Now imagine three of these bars. They are stacked on top of each other and pinned through their center. Each bar can spin independently. Looking at them like a clock hanging on a wall, the position of the bars determine which bar is prioritized over the other. So an eleven o'clock position would have priority over a nine o'clock position, and a one o'clock position would have priority over a three o'clock position. The bars cannot hold the same position because it's not humanly possible to prioritize two things at once.

The twelve o'clock position is what everything hangs on. There is a nail that holds everything up, and stops the bars from reaching the twelve o'clock position. The twelve o'clock position is held by the Anointed One, Jesus Christ. No one can change or move something into that space. He is the priority regardless of beliefs. The nail is a reminder of His testimony.

These three bars represent how an individual expresses themselves externally. One side of the bars represents the flesh and blood of the being, the other side represents their spiritual being. They are pinned to and controlled by the soul.

The soul (mind, emotions, will) is tethered to, and expressed through our bodies in 3 ways: gifts (ability), emotions (heart), and bodies (location). These "tethers" stretch to the earthly body and to the spiritual body. This makes 6 ends in total.

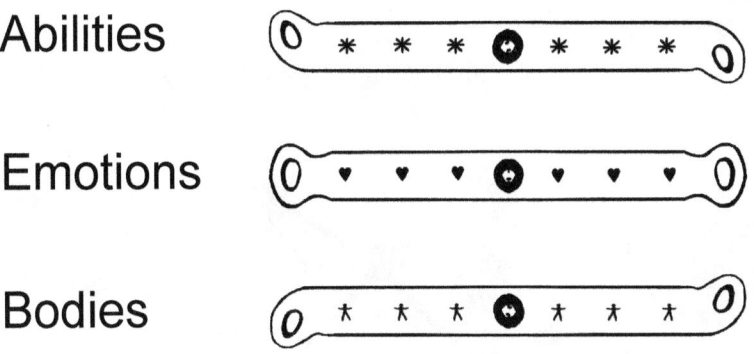

The 3 tethers of the soul: Abilities, Emotions, Bodies (respectively)

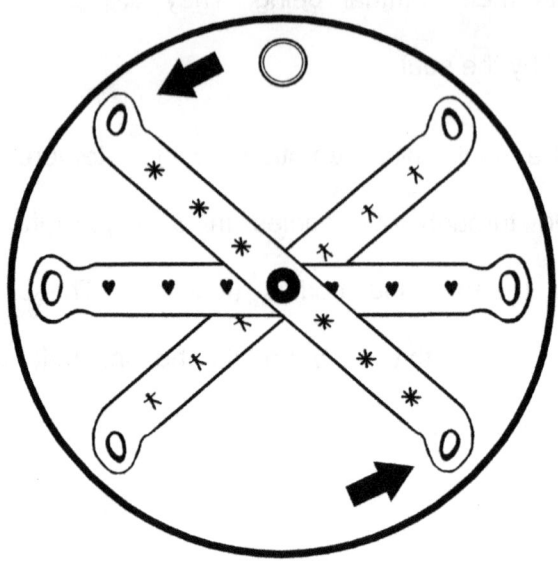

Tethers pinned at the center spin freely

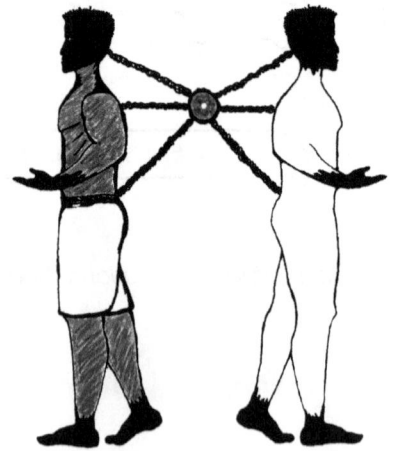

Tethers revisited: Physical body (left) & spiritual body (right) connected by the soul (center)

When we are born into this world we are given abilities. Abilities are given to everyone according to God's will. Some abilities are recognized as gifts and talents. There are abilities that manifest in "everyday" environments like social skills, emotional intelligence, creativity, intellect, athletic ability, etc. Everything you are born with is an ability when you submit them to the Lord. That includes the abilities that worldly cultures would consider a "disability." God wastes nothing.

Then there are abilities that are more spiritual in their nature. These abilities may need more intent in order to be drawn out of a person. These gifts include the ability to prophesy, minister, teach, exhort, rule, heal, perform miracles, discern spirits, speak in diverse tongues, interpret tongues, be charitable, be merciful, be wise, be exceedingly knowledgeable, be faithful, and be apostolic.

Some of these can be learned (to a degree), but people are custom made for their role in the Body of Christ. Being a good steward over what you've been given is key. To steward what God has given you well, you need to look to

God. Faithfully submitting your abilities to His will is a sure way to know that what has been given will not be squandered. From my experience and observation, we are given more than we know. Many people have "untapped" abilities.

Without God's guidance in using our abilities, the journey will be burden-filled with many fruitless experiences. With God's guidance the journey will be difficult, but with many fruitful experiences and a perspective that is reflective of God's Spirit.

God's Spirit brings love, joy, peace, patience, kindness, goodness, faithfulness, gentleness, and self-control; these things do not come from the spirit of this world (Galatians 5:22-23). With God's guidance the overflow of truly good fruit that occurs in your life will spread to the people around you, and hopefully, the people around them. Asking God to order our steps is where true purpose and fulfillment step in. With His guidance, everything we are will be used lovingly and effectively. This will be beneficial for everyone involved.

Regarding the flesh and blood end of the three tethers, I believe our abilities should be the highest priority. They are a major component in fulfilling the assignments that God has chosen for our lives. When we follow God's direction, our gifts and talents will exalt Him and expose others to His glory.

At the same time He will supply our physical, mental, and emotional needs. **The blessings that come will continually increase beyond what could be understood** and reach beyond our immediate circles (2 Corinthians 9:6-10). This does not mean once we find our gifts we just run with them. A continued, submitted relationship with God keeps us on the right path.

Requesting His grace, mercy, and provision to fulfill what He is calling us to do is a *daily* requirement. This is true for every part of our being, not just our abilities. Imagine a king's counsel or a president's cabinet operating for months or years without touching base or getting the leader's approval. In many cases "heads would roll."

The next bar is our emotions. This should be a middle priority in this world and the spiritual world. We have to put our emotions under our purpose, otherwise we could be distracted from fulfilling our calling well. This doesn't mean we should be emotionally numb, it means we shouldn't be controlled by our emotions.

God should have our heart, so our emotions should be submitted to His will for our lives. Emotions can work with or against us, so therefore they need to be understood in both bodies. This helps with consistency and stability. We have to share our emotional experiences with our Heavenly Father and receive His good counsel.

He will guide and supply us with the means to navigate our experiences and find emotional stability in them. This can include counsel from professionals, connecting with a God loving community, and council directly from the Holy Spirit. We should prioritize our emotions over our physical bodies because **if we can control our emotions then we can have better control over our bodies** (Proverbs 25:28).

Our flesh and blood bodies are the least intelligent and least capable part of our being, respectfully. Which is why it is the bottom priority on the flesh and blood side. Our earthly body's location doesn't matter if we are following God's guidance. If we have submitted and sought His counsel regarding our abilities and emotions, then our physical location should be appointed by Him. Which means we will be equipped to handle whatever environment we find ourselves in and He will be exalted. In addition, our fleshly bodies only last for a very short season in the scope of eternity. How we share ourselves through our abilities and emotions have eternal imprints.

On the other side of these bars is the spiritual side. They are solid bars, so a position change in the physical priority will yield an opposite direction in the spiritual priority. The location of the spiritual body is the most relevant because it resides in a higher dimension. This means the location of the spirit will have a "trickle-down effect" on everything, spiritually and in the flesh and blood.

The location of the spiritual body is more important than emotions because it will determine how close we are to the presence of God. Being in His presence helps us when we are weak everywhere else. We are told to protect our hearts and God is THE protector. So we want our spirit to be surrounded by godly things. Darkness, evil, and everything associated with those are powerless in the presence of God. **This is why when Satan had the thought to betray God he had to go away**, and meet with the other fallen angels elsewhere (Isaiah 14:12-15).

When flesh returns to dust, the soul resides in the spiritual body. **Spiritual bodies are designed to live for eternity** (1 Corinthians 15:51-53). When we are in the presence of God our abilities and emotions are not as significant as they are elsewhere. **Being in God's presence is being in the presence of unimaginable glory and majesty** (Jude 24-25).

The next bar on the spiritual side of our being, are emotions. As said earlier, they are the middle priority. Emotions seem to have the power to "tip the scales" in many scenarios. This makes emotions important enough to monitor closely, but they are too unreliable in the scope of making good decisions to make them the top priority. Emotions must be disciplined by the being bearing the emotions. This discipline is aided by bringing our feelings to the Father so He can help us sort them out.

At times you may feel far from God, but that doesn't mean He is far from you. Satan may have felt disloyalty and distance in his heart in the presence of God, but the act of creating distance and the act of betrayal is what sealed his fate. Satan allowed his emotions to undermine everything he knew, including his logic and location. God knows everything and could have removed Satan instantaneously as soon as he thought about betrayal, but He gave Lucifer and the other angels a chance to make a choice. I believe it's possible that if they made the choice to stay in God's presence and repent, things could have gone differently.

While we are alive on this Earth our gifts and talents should be the lowest priority on the spiritual side of our being. This can sound confusing, but let's walk through this. While we are flesh and blood beings, our abilities should be used to spread the good news of Christ and display the character that God created us to be. Although they may be spiritual actions or occurrences, they are brought into the world by our flesh. That is why on the flesh and blood side they are the top priority of the three. Spiritually, if our spirit is surrounded by unclean things and our emotions are unchecked, our gifts and talents are not going to be very useful (in a godly way) anywhere.

So, as we walk through life we want our spiritual body to be filled with and led by the Holy Spirit, which takes proximity (location) and obedience (submitted emotions). The power in which a spirit led person moves is not from themselves, it is by the power of the Holy Spirit. Their spiritual environment should be filled with and surrounded by God and godly things.

The desire and ability to use our gifts and talents to serve God is also given by Him. If a person were to read the Bible, ask God for direction, and then act out the direction by their own strength and desire, that person would eventually burn out. That commonly comes with a significant amount of negative fallout. This is because the things that God asks us to do require His strength, His mind, His heart, and ultimately His presence.

We should pray for Him to bless us with His strength while admitting our weakness. We should pray for His mind so we can operate by His knowledge and wisdom, not our own. We should pray for His heart, because our natural desires are carnal and unrighteous. When we receive Jesus, Jesus sends us His Spirit to live in us. So He is always present with a believer.

Our emotions should be submitted to God's will in the flesh and spirit, which will teach us self control. Our physical location should be ordered by God, therefore we can stand firm on Him no matter where we find ourselves. Our gifts and talents are in good use when our spirit and emotions are in alignment with God's will. All of these things begin with our willingness to follow Jesus, and are accomplished through the guidance and power of the Holy Spirit.

Without giving God control, there is nothing we can do to properly set our orientation. There is very little understanding of which side is up or which side is down. The priorities are out of order, and we cannot sustain balance or peace in our lives.

When you accept the gift of salvation, it comes with an ability to understand the Word of God through the guidance of the Holy Spirit. Like any ability, the strength of that ability will be increased through diligent studying and application (exercise). This is where the orientations of the tethers begin to shift.

The shift comes because now we are spiritually aware and walking with God as our "True North." When God has control, He can get things oriented because we asked Him to align our being with His. Not only is God our "north star," but He also helps us hold that orientation in place so we can sustain stability. God is good.

This is another revelation that God is more than a man. He has the knowledge and authority over everything we know and more. The amazing part is that with everything He is, He gives us so much time, attention, resources, and most of all, love. Many men in positions of power struggle with showing their loved one's love. God loves everyone more than we can understand, even the people that reject and rebel against Him. His majesty is unsurpassed in every way.

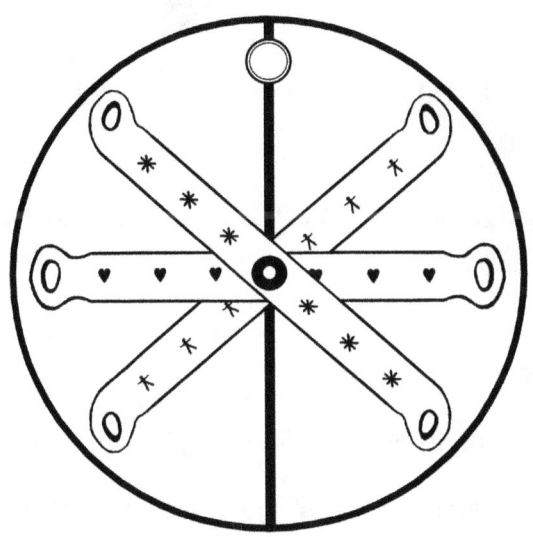

Earthly priorities (left), Spiritual priorities (right)

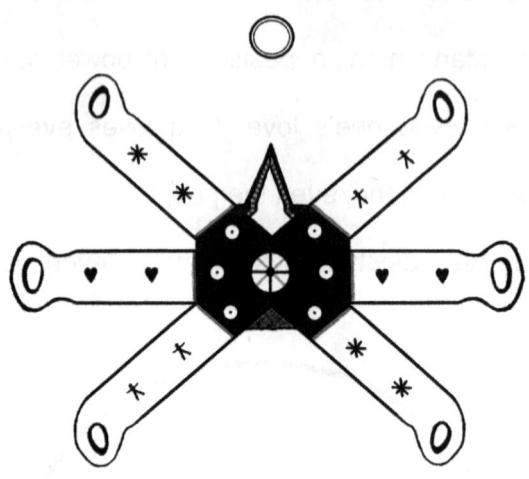

Priorities aligned & locked in place according to true north

Light & Death

Do not let death discourage you from life. Grief, depression, and survivors' guilt are natural reactions to tragedy. When we lose someone we love it feels like we lose a part of us. This is because when you love someone, you are sharing light between your souls. Two lights combined are brighter than one. So, when one leaves the other grieves that missing light of life.

Know that the light of God shines brighter than anything we can imagine, and it is everlasting. That is how **He**

can mend broken hearts and find lost souls (Psalms 34:18). There is nothing that the Lord cannot overcome, including death. The Lord is not withholding. He will help us overcome the sorrows and pain of life and death. A relationship with the Lord is how we can find the strength to go on in good spirit. Broken things cannot fix broken things, and the Lord is not broken.

The Lord brings peace that this world cannot. Seek His face and go on living. This is how we honor and respect the light that is no longer with us. There is a time to grieve and mourn, and there is also a time for healing and joy in your life. **Do not** allow sorrow to **cover your light** with darkness (Matthew 5:14-16).

Suicide is a common occurance that is usually tragic and tramatic. Whether it be by accident, for personal reasons, or to save another person's life, a choice was made. What we do know is that we don't know what others think, feel, or experience. Be very cautious in labeling these situations. Let the dead lay and do not judge things that you do not understand.

When it comes to loss please take time to grieve. We all grieve differently and it is a process. Unprocessed or misguided grief can lead to paths of destruction. Some of my most intimate times with God were during my hardest times. He was there with me in my pain, confusion, anger, frustration, and deep sorrow.

I have felt His presence in the midst of the deepest sorrow; His presence is enough to overcome it all. I am forever grateful for those experiences. They allow me to bear witness to His faithfulness and His goodness. You can ask Jesus to walk you through or carry you through the process of grieving. He knows what you are going through. **The Lord is close to the brokenhearted** (Psalms 34:18).

Plain and Simple

Repent. To repent is not just confessing and/or feeling sorry for an offense (sin). It is the act of turning away from the sin and turning towards God. Repentance is possible when we pray for a heart and mind that no longer desires to repeat sins. We can only truly defeat sin by receiving the gift of salvation from Jesus Christ. Be glad that there is an opportunity to repent and be forgiven.

A healthy relationship with God is available to everyone. **God has a specific purpose for all of his creations, and we are all wonderfully different** (1 Corinthians 12:12-27). Although none were created equal, all of mankind is highly valued by God. Pray that the Holy Spirit reminds you that God loves everyone, even the people you don't get along with.

Love is work. Sometimes to be good at our work we have to make a conscious effort to reject our comfortable and/or bad habits. Love is a process. **Do not grumble** at learning ways to improve yourself and your work (Colossians 3:23). Be thankful.

Live in truth. The truth may seem to make life difficult at times, but to lie is to speak death into your life . **There is no amount of money or "power" that is worth leading people away from God** (2 Peter 2:12-19). Manipulating people to think or act in the opposite direction of truth is a choice to lead them away from truth. Protect your mind and your heart from people and/or systems that perpetuate blatant contradictions between their words and actions.

Seeking peace is to seek the creator of the universe. Living in true peace is a better reward than anything mankind or other beings can offer.

Be good because our Heavenly Father asks you to, and reap rewards from heavenly places.

Every breath is a manifestation of God's grace. Remind yourself of the gifts of life by taking time to reflect on good experiences. Acknowledge God's love, grace, and mercy. Give thanks in all situations.

Know that you are actively worshiping someone or something today, and tomorrow is not promised. Many eyes remain closed to the light of today, and many will not witness the stars of tonight. Recognize your blessings and seize the opportunity to receive God's light; let it shine brilliantly from you. **The choice is yours** (Joshua 24:14-15).

Plain and Simple 274

The renewed soul

Chapter Reflection: More Than a Man

Intro

- Have you received the gift of salvation? If so, how has your journey been? Is there anything you would like to see?
- What are your thoughts on water baptism? Have you ever been baptized?
- Do you feel you have access to the Holy Spirit? Why or why not?
- Would you like access to the Holy Spirit?
- Do you pray? Why or why not?
- If you pray, have you seen your prayers answered?
- When you pray, do you feel like you need a physical object or person to pray to? Why or why not?

Three and One

- What do you think about the Holy Trinity?

- Have you ever prayed for a better understanding of the Holy Trinity?
- Are you a part of the body of Christ? How do you feel about that?

<u>New navigation</u>

- If you have received the gift of salvation, what about you changed?
- Is there a situation where you had to make a moral decision and you chose the "right" thing? How did it feel?
- How often do you experience these situations? What is your process for choosing a direction?
- Do you think your process is reliable for producing morally good results? Why or why not?

<u>True North</u>

- Currently, how are your three tethers organized physically and spiritually?
- Are you happy with this order? Why?
- What do you think are your "natural" abilities? Do you use them?

- ❖ If applicable, how do you feel when you're using your natural talents?
- ❖ If you believe in spiritual talents, do you think you have any? What are they?

Calibrated Compass

- ❖ What do you use as your true north?
- ❖ Do you try to hold your life together or do you ask for help? Why?
- ❖ What areas in your life do you think are sustainable? What areas do you need help in?
- ❖ What are your top six priorities? Which ones have you asked God to take control over?

Light & Death

- ❖ How do you cope with stress, grief, depression, anger, or guilt?
- ❖ Have you ever considered professional and/or spiritual guidance on these matters?
- ❖ Define freedom in your own words.

❖ If you were to apply your definition of freedom to your life, what would that look like? Be specific.

Plain and Simple

❖ Where are you mentally and spiritually?

Book Reflection

- ❖ What do you think is more important than finding internal peace?
- ❖ How much time in your day do you dedicate to understanding yourself?
- ❖ If all your obligations were cleared, how would you want to spend your time?
- ❖ Knowing that we don't know how much time we have left as individuals, do you think you need to reprioritize how you spend your time? If so, how?

Feel free to revisit your answers throughout the book and expand on your thoughts and reflections.

Epilogue

The Book Title

The title, *Carbon Copies: Shadows of the Almighty*, contains layers of analogies and meanings.

The main title, *Carbon Copies*, references the stationery and our elemental composition. The stationery analogy is that all of creation has imprints of God in some way or another. Like forms that use carbon paper, the imprint is not the original. The copy is a significantly imperfect impression of the original form. Although imperfect, the copy is clear enough to get the information contained in the original form. In short, *all* of creation is an indication of our Creator.

The elemental analogy points to the scientific understanding that all living things on earth are considered carbon-based lifeforms. So in a more literal sense, everything that is living is a carbon-based expression and/or impression of God and His Kingdom.

The graphic on the cover was made to symbolize the carbon atom. Carbon has an atomic number of six on the periodic table. It wasn't until everything was done when I realized the similarities between the cover graphic and the calibrated compass graphic in chapter nine.

The subtitle, *Shadows of the Almighty*, is an analogy relating to man being made in the image of God. Shadows are an indicator that something is present. They are not the substance of the thing, but bring awareness to the thing. Mankind is very unique compared to the rest of creation. In addition, considering that the spiritual world is more real than this material one, our material bodies are like shadows of our spiritual parts.

It is my hope and prayer that we become like His "shadows." Which would mean that we move how He moves, when He moves.

Receiving Salvation

I hope everyone becomes active in pursuing an intentional, healthy relationship with God. Just like an earthly relationship, your relationship with God starts with a conversation. God started the conversation when He spoke life into you. In response, you can reply by acknowledging Him, introducing yourself, and engaging in conversation. This conversation should be spoken in truth, with your heart, mind, and if possible, voice, focussed on Him.

To pray is to submit requests to God which is normally by way of conversation. Receiving the gift of salvation is a prayer of giving yourself to God in which He returns an eternity of living in, with, and for Him. True life is to be united with God. It is to live in the fullness of your creation and worship Him. His majesty and glory is unimaginable, and it will be experienced continually by those that choose Him.

You can receive the gift of salvation by praying a prayer that acknowledges the God of Abraham as God, proclaiming that Jesus Christ is Lord, Jesus gave His life to pay for your sins, and then rose from the dead by the power of God.

The prayer could be this or something similar: "Heavenly Father, I pray to you in the name of Jesus asking to be forgiven of my sins. I know that I am guilty of sin, and I want to turn away from a life of sin. I believe you sent your son, Jesus Christ, to live, die, and rise to live again, so I can be forgiven for my sins. I proclaim Jesus is Lord! I receive your gift of salvation, and I dedicate my entire being to you. Thank you Heavenly Father, thank you Jesus, Amen."

It is possible you may have heard or seen a variation of this prayer and that's ok. Here are some biblical references about receiving the gift of salvation for you to study:

- John 14:6
- John 11:25-26
- Romans 10:9-10
- Ephesians 2:8-10

The Writing Process

I believe this book is a gift from God to me and whoever receives the content. Becoming an author was not on my list of things to do until one very early morning I was awakened by some of the concepts discussed in the book. As they came into my mind, I felt the call to write them down. After some time had passed, I was reminded of what was written and the instruction was pretty clear to me; I was to write until I was told to rest.

From that day on it was a daily conversation in the form of prayer, questions, research, and new revelations flooding my mind while I tried my best to compose the work. I had to pause many times and digest the material that I had just written because the concepts, connections, and revelations felt "beyond" me. There were several times when I questioned the material, but I was encouraged to continue writing and told that there would be a time for validation and confirmation.

There were many rough drafts, edits, and reviews before any biblical references were connected. Adding the biblical references was a process. I wasn't a person who memorized a large amount of scripture, so I was a bit overwhelmed when I realized the amount of potential references there could have been. There was also content that I thought referenced scripture that did not; which caused me to humble myself and hit that delete button. I believe I was led to remove some of the accurate references as well. It was a healthy process of learning how to be led by the Spirit and receive discipline with gratitude.

The next steps were composed of editing for structure, grammar, and compassion...repeatedly. The images came after the text was relatively in order. I don't consider myself an artist, but I believe God is pleased with my effort.

All that to say, I believe I was led by the Holy Spirit throughout the process of writing this book. The biblical subjects and theologies discussed were significantly dormant to my conscience when I started. I say conscious because I regularly read the Bible for many years prior to writing the book, but I was not fully aware of the knowledge my being had been exposed to. The best way I can describe it is that the information was being "unpacked" in my brain while I was writing, which was a startling and exciting experience.

I know there is a lot more for me to learn. My understanding at this point is that it is impossible for us (humans) to fully comprehend the magnificence of God and His given Word. Even though we may never fully understand Him, we should never cease seeking Him, His love, His wisdom, His peace, and His purpose for our lives.

Epilogue

About the Author

Ryan Harris is devoted to Jesus Christ and believes that everyone can have access to The Kingdom of Heaven. He has been blessed with an open heart and curious mind that led him down many paths personally and professionally. These experiences created opportunities for him to observe and understand (to an extent) the complexities of the human perspective and experience. Ryan considers himself a "jack of all trades, master of none," so he is not a stranger to applying theory to practice. He acknowledges that although his walk may not have been a straight one, nothing he has experienced is or will be wasted (by the wisdom of God).

Ryan is a part of a family of four composed of him, his wife, and two daughters. As an entrepreneur, he has goals to create collaborative spaces that bring communities together through common interests such as motorsports and STEAM (Science, Technology, Engineering, Art, Math) related subjects. Ultimately, Ryan's life-long commitment is to walk the path God created for him and be the husband, father, family member, friend, and person God calls him to be.

Share Your Thoughts

I hope you enjoyed the book. If you'd like to share your story or offer feedback regarding the book, you can do so on my website RHarrisWrites.com. If you're interested in finding out more about the author, current projects, and upcoming events; you can find those on the website as well.

Peace, R. H.

SCAN HERE FOR

R.HARRIS WRITES
WEBSITE

www.ingramcontent.com/pod-product-compliance
Lightning Source LLC
Chambersburg PA
CBHW071111160426
43196CB00013B/2532